T0304950

CONVERSATION STARTERS for DIRECT WORK with CHILDREN and YOUNG PEOPLE

by the same author

Direct Work with Family Groups
Simple, Fun Ideas to Aid Engagement and Assessment and Enable Positive Change
Audrey Tait and Helen Wosu
ISBN 978 1 84905 554 3
eISBN 978 0 85700 986 9
Part of the Practical Guides for Direct Work *series*

Direct Work with Vulnerable Children
Playful Activities and Strategies for Communication
Audrey Tait and Helen Wosu
ISBN 978 1 84905 319 8
eISBN 978 0 85700 661 5
Part of the Practical Guides for Direct Work *series*

of related interest

Giving Children a Voice
A Step-by-Step Guide to Promoting Child-Centred Practice
Sam Frankel
ISBN 978 1 78592 278 7
eISBN 978 1 78450 578 3

Helping Children to Tell About Sexual Abuse
Guidance for Helpers
Rosaleen McElvaney
ISBN 978 1 84905 712 7
eISBN 978 1 78450 235 5

A Practical Guide to Early Intervention and Family Support
Assessing Needs and Building Resilience in Families Affected
by Parental Mental Health Problems or Substance Misuse
Emma Sawyer and Sheryl Burton
ISBN 978 1 90939 121 5
eISBN 978 1 90939 130 7

CONVERSATION STARTERS

for DIRECT WORK with
CHILDREN and YOUNG PEOPLE

Guidance and Activities for
Talking About Difficult Subjects

AUDREY TAIT and BECKY DUNN

Jessica Kingsley *Publishers*
London and Philadelphia

First published in 2018
by Jessica Kingsley Publishers
73 Collier Street
London N1 9BE, UK
and
400 Market Street, Suite 400
Philadelphia, PA 19106, USA

www.jkp.com

Copyright © Audrey Tait and Becky Dunn 2018

All rights reserved. No part of this publication may be reproduced in any material form (including photocopying, storing in any medium by electronic means or transmitting) without the written permission of the copyright owner except in accordance with the provisions of the law or under terms of a licence issued in the UK by the Copyright Licensing Agency Ltd. www.cla.co.uk or in overseas territories by the relevant reproduction rights organisation, for details see www.ifrro.org. Applications for the copyright owner's written permission to reproduce any part of this publication should be addressed to the publisher.

Warning: The doing of an unauthorised act in relation to a copyright work may result in both a civil claim for damages and criminal prosecution.

Library of Congress Cataloging in Publication Data
A CIP catalog record for this book is available from the Library of Congress

British Library Cataloguing in Publication Data
A CIP catalogue record for this book is available from the British Library

ISBN 978 1 78592 287 9
eISBN 978 1 78450 593 6

Printed and bound in Great Britain

Contents

Acknowledgements

The authors would like to dedicate this book, and say thank you, to the children and families that we have met who often face multiple adversities in their lives. It is our privilege to be given the opportunity to work with you. We also thank our colleagues and our manager Andy McWhirter for the invaluable support they have offered us, and encouragement in writing this book.

We also want to thank the numbers of artists who helped make this book come alive through your pictures – S. Cathcart, Bob Dunn and those children who contributed but who have not been named to protect their anonymity.

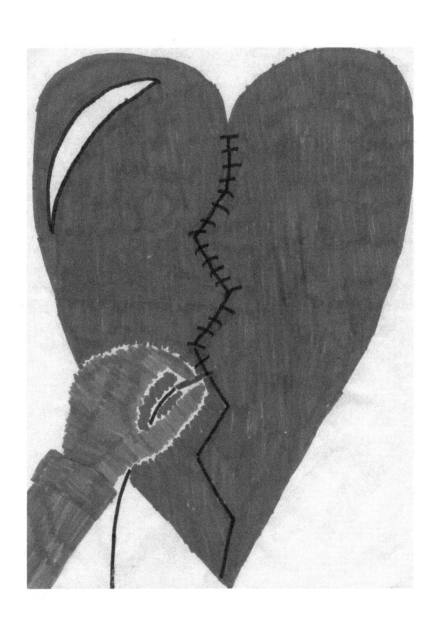

Chapter 1

Introduction

If you have spent time around children, you will undoubtedly have found yourself in one of those difficult moments when you have no idea how to explain something to a child. Whether this is about the finer details of puberty or the origins of the universe, providing an explanation off the top of your head can be challenging. When it comes to more difficult and sensitive subjects, and where emotions may be fraught, it is perhaps no surprise that some adults avoid the subject altogether. Often the decision not to talk to children about difficult subjects is motivated by the desire to protect them from the pain of the truth.

Yet children have a right to know about matters that affect their lives, and need to be supported to understand them. Rather than protecting a child, a lack of communication may have the opposite effect. Children may be aware that something is wrong and use their imagination to erroneously fill in the gaps. They may overhear adult discussion or rumours in the community, and have to deal with this alone, aware that they were not meant to know and therefore unable to divulge that they are aware of the information. In addition, children have a right to have their views heard and their wishes taken into account. This cannot be done in a meaningful way unless the child is provided with all the information required to make a decision (for the purposes of this book, the term 'child' refers to a person up to the age of 16 years).

The authors have experience of trying to talk to children about a number of difficult subjects. Despite recognising that children have the right to be informed, we know it can be hard to give children information, particularly when it may cause them distress. We also recognise that it can be hard to know how to approach a subject, what words to use and how to explain something in a way that is appropriate to the developmental stage of the child. It is out of this experience that we came to write this book, hoping that we would be able to support others to feel more equipped to talk to children.

The main part of the book is divided into chapters organised by subject headings. As well as information, there are activities to support conversation, because we know that play is both the doorway to the child's world, and is also a non-direct (and therefore non-threatening) way of communicating. Practice examples are also found throughout the book, and are anonymised so as to protect the identity of the children and families in question. The word 'I' is also used in these examples to provide further anonymity.

Chapter 2

Preparation

What you say to children when discussing a difficult subject with them is as important as the way in which this is done. Sometimes you may not have much time to prepare, but below we have detailed what is helpful to consider before speaking to a child.

Venue

The venue you choose will depend on the child, their developmental stage and what is practical. Venues are not neutral, however; they will elicit particular memories and emotions for children. For example, someone might choose the head teacher's office in a school because it is quiet and a place where you and a child will not be disturbed. However, for some children this room will be a place where they or others are sent when in trouble, and even if this is not the case the head teacher's office is a social space associated with power. How you position yourself in the room is also important. As adults, we have a level of authority as well as generally being taller and bigger than children, therefore we would suggest sitting at a level with the child. Often this can involve sitting on the floor alongside them or ensuring that you are at the same eye level as the child. You may also want to think about the child being seated nearer the door, particularly if you are not a familiar adult to them, as this allows them to leave easily if they wish to. Again, if you are not a familiar adult to the child, it is important that the child is made aware of where their safe adult is. The authors would tend to arrange in these circumstances for the safe adult to bring the child to where you are, and spend time speaking with you so the child can see that the safe adult knows you and is comfortable with you. We would then ask permission from the child for their safe adult to leave, making them aware of where their safe adult will be should they wish to go and find them.

Who will speak to the child?

One of the other decisions that needs to be made is who will give the information to the child, and who else, if anyone, will be present. If possible, the information should be given to the child by a familiar and safe adult, but sometimes this cannot be achieved for various reasons. If the most familiar and safe adult feels unable to supply the information, you may agree that they are at least present and able to support the child whilst someone else gives them information. Likewise, the familiar and safe adult may desire to have someone else present to support them. In general, it is advisable to keep numbers to no more than two adults as this in itself can be imposing to the child.

Agreeing what to say

The process of coming to an agreement about what information is to be given can take time. Adults may wish to protect children from having certain information or it may be necessary to protect the confidentiality of another person. Where there is resistance from the adult(s) who is responsible for the child, they may need support and time to get to a place where they can understand the reasons for the child knowing. Be aware that where difficult information needs to be shared, it is possible that family members are themselves having to come to terms with or process information. They might also need support and sensitivity on the part of those around them. This could involve co-working with services for adults, such as counselling.

Key to making the decision about what to say is gaining an understanding of what the child already knows. This may be because people have already given them information, which may be appropriate, but bear in mind it may also have been inaccurate. The authors have experience of children being told incorrect information in order to present the adults in a better light; for example, that a parent is away working rather than in prison, or words have been used that do not correctly detail what is happening; for example, a parent is 'ill' rather than has issues with problematic substance use. Just because a child has been given information, don't assume that they understand it. For example, it can be hard for a young child to understand that they may be prescribed drugs when unwell, but may not be able to live with a family member because that family member takes prescribed drugs (and misuses them). The key to this is to never assume what a child knows, or what their understanding of this is. Check this out with children by asking them to tell you what they think it means. Avoid saying things like 'do you understand?' as this is a closed question that may elicit a 'yes' even if the child doesn't understand. 'Can you tell me about it?' is a better question.

A note on the issue of time pressures

When I (Audrey) train social workers, a barrier to direct work that I come across is the pressure people are under in terms of case work and a feeling of 'I don't have time.' I do empathise with this, working in a practice team myself. However, I can't agree with it. Sessions take the same amount of time as a home visit and offer children a valuable service and assessment opportunity. Ultimately, you are more effective in protecting children when you spend time with them and offer them a relationship.

What to bring

Each activity within the book contains details of what you will need in order to do that activity. Beyond this, there are some key items you may wish to bring. We have listed these below:

- pens and paper

- blank cards and stamps (the child may wish to write a card to someone after they have been given the information, e.g. a parent in prison, a sick relative, etc.)

- a stress ball/playdough (something that the child can manipulate in their hands if feeling anxious)

- a snack and a drink (this is a nurturing act and demonstrates that you can recognise and meet a child's needs, and therefore builds trust)

- a game or something similar to play with at the end of the session – you will want a few choices

- a diary (writing down in front of the child when you will next see them makes it concrete that you will see them again and when that will be, and children tend to like to see their name in your diary)

- tissues

- a teddy or puppet to cuddle

- a few nurturing story books to choose from and possibly one or two about the subject in question

- an emotional literacy activity

- depending on the venue, blankets and pillows to create a soft and comforting environment.

Talking with the child

Whatever the subject is, you need to go at the pace of the child. This might mean that you only start to discuss the issue with them. The way you will know that the pace is too fast includes a child having lots of questions, showing through their body language that they have had enough or by them simply choosing to end the time you have with them. Children tend to dip in and out of subjects, especially when stressful; the skill is to embrace and foster this.

The timing of giving the child information may be something that you have little control over, or it may be something that you can completely control. A general rule would be that talking to children about difficult subjects when they are tired or late at night is not ideal, because they will find it harder to process the information, may be more emotionally sensitive and may lie awake thinking about this at bedtime. Ideally, you will choose a time in which the child can be supported before, during and after.

As information is being given, it is important the child is given space to respond. Statements such as 'I'm wondering what you think/feel about that' or 'How is that to hear?' invite a child to give their thoughts and feelings. Silence is a powerful but underused tool. Be careful to give children the time to respond to such statements, rather than jumping in quickly if no immediate answer is provided. Whilst it can be uncomfortable, the child will need time to process what has been said, and then time to identify their thoughts and feelings in response to this. If the subject is emotive or difficult, then they will be doing this in the context of experiencing a number of different emotions. It is tempting to allow negative behaviour from a child in the context of having given the child difficult information because we feel empathy for the child's situation. However, it is important to maintain boundaries in order to contain the behaviour that the child is displaying, as you normally would. This will help the child to feel safe both physically and emotionally.

Supporting the child after

For children who are able to reflect on what they need, you may be able to ask a child what they need from you or other people at the end of your discussion, using questions such as 'Who can help you?' and 'What can they do?' You may also ask direct questions such as 'Do you need a cuddle…who do you need it from?

You may also ask a child what they would like to do next. This might include doing some exercise, playing with friends or simply returning to the familiarity of their usual routine. However, many children will find it difficult to identify what they need or want, or will be unable to articulate it. At times of stress, children will regress in terms of their processing and may need choices in order to make decisions. You might say something such as 'What do you think? Do we need to go outside and play with a ball for a while or will we go to the library and have a quiet story?'

Don't be surprised if there is no obvious and immediate reaction to what you have discussed with them. Children may choose to play and seem unaffected by the difficult topic of conversation. This is entirely normal, and reflects how children process information. It is likely that they will come back to their chosen adult at a later time with questions or wishing to continue the conversation. Another common reaction is either an increase in energy/activity or the need to sleep. These can both be indicators of stress.

After a difficult conversation, it can be helpful to tell the child that you would like to let key people know that this conversation has happened in order that they can be aware of what is happening for the child. Seeking the child's permission to do this is important. Sometimes children will not want people to know for fear of shame and stigma, and therefore it is worth exploring any resistance to a key person being informed. This might be explored using open statements such as 'Help me understand your reason for not wanting…to know' or 'I am curious/wondering…'

It is also helpful to think about next steps with a child. This might include them identifying what safe adults they could go to with any questions or worries, when you will see them again, what you will be doing with regard to any questions they might have and what they might wish to do with the information they have been given. The Safe Hands activity below can help with this. You might also help children to think about what they might want to say/not say to their friends. Younger children will not necessarily appreciate that there could be negative consequences to telling people. A useful approach is to help the child to think about what information they know about people they only know a little, in comparison to what they know about a very close friend or family member. This can help children think about who they choose to tell information to, and how much information they give to that person. You might consider ensuring that the child knows how to contact you if they do have anything they need to check out with you before you see them again. A little credit card-sized piece of paper or card could be given to the child with your details on, so that they can give this to an adult when they want to contact you/use it to contact you themselves.

Activity: Safe Hands
Purpose

- To help you find out from a child the people in his/her world who they feel can keep them safe.

What you will need

- lots of paper, at least A4 size
- baby wipes or access to a wash basin
- a safe space to work in

- good-quality felt tips. (Most children I meet like coloured pens. It is important that they all work and are of nice quality. From a child's perspective, if they are unhappy and stressed to begin with, their favourite colour of pen not working can tip the balance from this being a fun thing to do, to something they are only doing because we have asked them to. We are asking a child to produce something for us. Let us respect their efforts by giving them good materials. Children *do* notice and so do any professionals you may later show their work to.)

What to do

1. To begin, allow free play. Enjoy the pens and paper, talk about the colours and make your own picture. It is important to join in as this promotes a feeling of togetherness and gives you common ground. Try and draw simple things that the child could easily draw. If you produce pictures that are too adult or impressive, the child will tend to be inhibited in their work or become more interested in your pictures. What you want is free flowing and relaxed art production from the young person.

2. The next step is to introduce the idea of drawing round each other's hands. You need to judge the point when the production of pictures is decreasing but the child has not yet got fed up with the pens. Introduce it with playfulness and enthusiasm. You might say, with a smile on your face and excitement in your voice, 'Hey! I've got a good idea. Let's draw around each other's hands.' I (Audrey) have never had a child say no. By this time, I have built up my communication with the child, they have experienced me as a helpful and fun adult, so they are now happy to meet my need to direct the play. This is why it is important to have free play at the start.

3. Suggest that the child draws round your hand first. This gives the message, 'I trust you.' It also feels safer for the child. Remember that they might not trust adults and/or be dealing with trauma, so drawing round hands is initiating physical contact. This is a big deal for some children, so go gently.

Once your hand is drawn, you could say: 'You know when I was a little girl, people used to hold my hand when we crossed the road to keep me safe.' All you are doing by saying this is introducing the idea of safe adults.

4. Then draw around the child's hands. Have as much fun as possible and give lots of compliments. Maybe do a couple of drawings round hands. You will need to judge how much the child is enjoying it and the right time to take the next step: 'I know, we could write the names of the people who keep us safe on the fingers of the hands. That would be pretty cool.' Offer to write on behalf of the child. Writing can be hard work for some children and you don't want them to disengage. You could ask the child who they like to hold hands with when watching a scary bit on television, or when they are at the dentist, or crossing a road and so on. Remember to ask about a variety of settings. It may be that Granny is the safest person in the child's life but she is housebound and can't hold hands crossing the road. Your assessment will only be as good as the opportunities you give, so give it thought. Next, ask the child which finger you will use for each person, and which colour you will use to write their name.

5. To finish up, go back to free play/drawing at the end of the session. Have a tidy-up ritual and, during this, talk about the safe hand picture, and how interesting it is, and how it helps you to learn about the child's family. Then ask permission to keep it for a little while so that you can photocopy it or if you can, photocopy it whilst with the child. If you are going to use this for a professional purpose, ensure that you ask the child's permission before using it.

Chapter 3

Partnership Working

We firmly believe that working hand in hand as a team with everybody who cares for/looks after the child is the best and most effective way to work. It is, however, not always as easy as it sounds.

Everybody will have their own specialism/focus and relationship with the child, and it is natural that everybody will be passionate about their particular specialism – whether that be the parent who knows their child best, or a professional with a particular focus. All this passion and difference in perspective can be challenging as the example below shows.

I (Audrey) went to see a secondary school head teacher to update them on the fact that the child had disclosed that they had been mistreated by an adult in their family. I explained that I would need to speak to the adult and that this would not be an easy conversation, so it was possible that the child would be under stress in the next few days. I asked if the guidance teacher could 'check in' with the child daily. The head teacher was concerned and had a very caring attitude, and assured me that this would happen. He then said, 'As long as this doesn't interfere with their education, we will be okay.' I was slightly taken aback by this statement. I didn't disagree that education was important but from my perspective as a social worker I was more concerned about the child's safety and their emotional health. Education at that point was not really on my agenda! Neither of us was wrong, we just had different priorities.

To my mind, this is a clear argument for partnership working because if everyone has a slightly different priority, then every aspect of the child's world and their development will be held as important. Nothing will be overlooked or forgotten.

The skill is in all the adults working together and agreeing that sometimes, for a short while, one aspect of the child's care will take precedence over another.

Talking to children about something challenging is a good example. There is never a good time for someone to die, for a loved one to become critically ill or for a caregiver to relapse in their substance use. We can all accept that and pull together at times of crisis to support a child. But when it is a planned conversation about something hard, there will always be a reason not to do it. Parents will often say things like, 'Not yet – I am not strong enough, I need to be in the right place, I don't want to upset them.' Education professionals may say, 'Exams or tests are coming up, it's not a good time.' Health workers may say, 'Mum is due her baby. If we start bringing this up now, that is going to give her more to cope with.' Social workers might say, 'He is only just settling into his placement. Let's get his routines established and him feeling safe before we give him more difficult things to cope with.'

It is likely that all of the above arguments are valid. This may be to differing degrees at different times. But sometimes these reasons (or similar ones) are not really what is behind the desire for a delay. Usually there are a few things going on:

- People do not wish to feel that they have caused upset and distress even when they know that the child is already experiencing this, and that talking about it should help.

- People consciously, or subconsciously, don't want to acknowledge that the child is having to deal with difficult things. Particularly when these are things that adults find hard, and we believe that children shouldn't have to cope with them.

- People are afraid that they may not cope with the child's reaction to the information, either on an emotional or a practical level.

The key to all this is that if you develop good rapport and support within the team around the child then you will all be able to challenge each other in a way that allows things to get done, and you will be able to support each other. Ultimately, the child will reap the benefits.

So how do you do that?

Here is the good news – it is not rocket science – it is all about relationships! Here are a few of our top tips to foster working in partnership:

- Meet regularly as a group – a team around the child.

- Take time to have a little bit of social interaction with each other, even just a few minutes asking about each other's work, holidays, etc.

- Outside meetings, keep in touch with each other regularly by phone or email. Foster your relationships with individual members of the group.

- Learn about each other's roles, particularly in relation to knowledge of the child. Show respect for each other's expertise or each other's skills – that might be the parent's intimate knowledge of their child or the health professional's understanding of the child's medical condition.

- Share positive information about what you have been doing with the child. Anecdotal stories in the context of stressful times can help to see the bigger picture for the child, whether that be a trip the child enjoyed going on or something the child said.

- Foster a culture (by doing it yourself) of being open and honest about your views and work through any disagreements.

- Be clear about who is doing what.

- Above all, remember that you all want the best for the child – the child is your common interest. I (Audrey) tend to help this along by saying things like, 'It's great to get everyone together – we are now "team [child's name]".' I ask people to tell the child that they are on the child's team and, for children who are old enough to understand, I like them to see us together. Occasionally I tell them, 'we are your team'.

Partnership working when preparing to talk about difficult subjects

The team needs to agree:

- who will tell the child

- who will support the person telling the child

- where and when this will happen

- on a common language/explanation that everyone in the team will use

- on a support plan for after the child has been told

- on how to update each other about the child's needs/reactions after this conversation.

Be aware and be clear that after the initial conversation, the child will choose whom they want to talk to. This might be a safe adult in their team but it may be someone outside their team. It is not uncommon for a child to tell a peer. You may therefore need to plan for how you will potentially support the child's peer group and answer any queries from other parents or professionals connected to peers.

Partnership working is hard – you are not going to get it right all the time. So, when it does go wrong, forgive yourselves, repair the damage and move forward. I find it is a whole lot easier when you work in the same area for a long time because when you form a new team you often know people already. You therefore have a kick start to the relationships. It can be unnerving, however, when the parents or other adults were once children you looked after (not that this makes us feel old!). Joking aside, it gives a sense of being part of a community both to the workers and to the families involved. In our experience this is always a positive thing and aids partnership working. The underlying message is simply that you care and have a shared history with that community.

Chapter 4

Talking to Children About Bullying

What is bullying?

Bullying can consist of many different things but mostly it's a combination of more than one behaviour. A child can be bullied by one other child or by a group. Here are some of the more common behaviours I would associate with bullying, but this list is not exhaustive.

Physical violence or aggression

Examples include pushing, hitting, kicking, spitting, using something to hurt someone or threatening physical violence, forcing a person into a fight, not letting someone pass, locking a person in somewhere, putting someone's head down a toilet, deliberately stamping on a foot, forcing someone to part from their possessions; for example, pulling their bag away from them or taking an item of clothing off them in an aggressive way.

Verbal or emotional abuse

Examples include name calling, chanting insults, shouting at, making threats or sending pictures of the child online with the purpose of embarrassing or humiliating the bullied child.

Excluding

Examples include refusing to play with or speak to the child or young person, making plans that include everyone apart from the person who is being bullied, changing plans and telling everyone except the bullied person or spreading rumours so the child becomes talked about or unpopular.

Controlling

Examples include taking the bullied child's lunch or money, making them complete another person's homework, forcing them to run errands or act on the bully's behalf, making threats against the bullied child's family or setting up situations so the bullied child gets into trouble with an adult.

It is important to remember that bullying can occur anywhere: it is no longer confined to the playground. The advent of social media has brought a whole new dimension to bullying. It is good to know, however, that the issues are now wildly acknowledged and **we** have found that the majority of schools that I work with are very good at spotting bullying and acting on it. It is also worth noting that in serious cases the police have powers, including in relation to online bullying.

But how do we talk about bullying to children and what can we do to help with bullying?

How to talk to children

There are plenty of books and materials out there to use. A top tip would be to begin this conversation even if you don't think you need to. In the same way that we talk to children about 'stranger danger', it is something that you need to revisit regularly as a 'check in' if you like.

As a social worker, when I am first getting to know a child and their family, it is one of the areas I always look at. I (Audrey) make sure that I ask the children and their parents separately if they have had any experience of bullying. Note that I do not say 'of being bullied' because I want to be open to the possibility that the child themselves might be the bully. At this point, it can be helpful to do a simple exercise around what bullying is. I tend to do this by asking everyone to draw a picture about bullying and then talk from there.

A child who is being bullied is probably able to recognise what is happening as bullying, unless it is in a subtler form. An example of this would be a child I worked with who thought that the bullies were his friends. The fact that these 'friends' had been physically hurting him and expecting him to do errands was, for him, part of the friendship. Sadly, he was so desperate to have friends and his self-esteem was so low, that he saw their behaviour as an acceptable trade-off. Someone who is doing the bullying may also not recognise that their behaviour is bullying, particularly when this is taking place online.

A key message that needs to be given when talking about bullying is that it is not acceptable. This is not something that children should have to put up with, and it should not be condoned if the child is the one bullying others. We would not tolerate being isolated, called names, assaulted or having our belongings taken in the workplace, yet many adults tolerate such behaviour for children, providing responses such as 'just ignore them'.

On the other hand, it can be tempting to want to jump in and problem solve when it comes to bullying. The most important thing you can do when talking to children about bullying is to listen to their experiences and how they are feeling. It is important too that children can feel in control of what is happening. Children frequently report that they do not speak to adults about bullying because they fear that the adults will make it worse by intervening in a way that does not help. Children who are being bullied will already feel out of control and frightened, and adults taking over the situation can simply exacerbate that. If the bullying is so serious that something has to be done immediately, it is important to share this with the child and allow them to have whatever control is possible in how this is done. It may be that you are able to explore with the child what they think can be done to minimise or stop the bullying, but before doing so it is important to get a really good feel for what life is like for the child.

When talking to children about bullying, try to establish the different ways in which it is taking place – the who, how, where, when and how often. You might want to find out what the hardest part of the bullying is, and what the child is scared of. Remember that bullying may take place both in the offline and online world. You will also want to know if the child has friends in the environment in which it is taking place, and if there are circumstances in which the bullying doesn't happen.

Children may struggle to understand why bullying is taking place, and may often blame themselves or see themselves in a negative light. Children need to be reassured that they are not to blame for being bullied, and it may help for the child to understand why people bully in the first place.

What we know is that people may bully for a number of reasons. For some children, this is because they have experienced being bullied themselves, either by other children or have been treated badly by adults. This can lead children to bully others whom they perceive as weaker than themselves. For other children bullying brings with it a feeling of being powerful and may lead to popularity within a group. Bullying can also be a result of jealousy of the person being bullied. At the root of all these reasons is the bully feeling unhappy and insecure. Providing a bullied child with this information can help the child to not blame themselves, but also can help a child to reclaim some of the 'power' they have psychologically given over to the bully.

As already noted, it common for children to struggle to tell a trusted adult that they are being bullied. Often this is because they believe that it will make the situation far worse for them. In some cases that worry could be accurate and as adults we should remember that, acknowledge it and commend any child who is brave enough to confide in us. However, there are some behaviours that might indicate bullying is taking place:

- unexplained bumps and bruises

- ripped clothes or bags – if this is unusual

- money going missing or a need to try and get money (this could also apply to cigarettes)

- extra treats going out of the cupboard, or a child not eating their sweets but always taking them to school. This could indicate that they need them for a bully who is demanding these things or being pacified by being given these

- a child being exceptionally hungry when they come home, which may indicate they have not had their lunch

- withdrawn behaviour

- a reluctance to go to sleep, or night disturbances

- a child rushing to the toilet immediately after they come home, which could indicate they don't want to use the toilet at school

- a lack of friends – this can indicate social exclusion or a child isolating themselves to keep safe

- anxiety or upset around social media. Becoming very stressed if asked to leave electronic devices for a short period; children who are being bullied via social media often have a desperate need to always see what is happening/being said, as they try to work out how to deal with this

- needing constant reassurance about their appearance or forcing themselves to diet or dress in a manner that you wouldn't normally associate with them

- general distress but the child being unable to articulate what is wrong.

Of course, some of these things could be attributed to the changes and challenges of growing up, or could be due to other things, but I would suggest that when you are considering what is wrong, do think about bullying.

How we can help

For a long time, I really struggled with this question partly because I always felt that I was failing, and never being effective enough in my ability to stop bullying. The harsh and unpalatable reality is that it's impossible to eradicate bullying, and trying to prevent it and stop it is a big challenge. When I worked with groups of children I felt relatively more empowered to deal with the issue of bullying as I made sure that we talked about it regularly, and I could work with the group so that there was less opportunity available. For example, I could use buddy systems, reward positive behaviour and, knowing the children well, it was easier to spot potential trouble. As a professional or parent around one child, it is difficult to have a sense of the space or the dynamic and you will tend to have only a small percentage of the information available. I came to the conclusion that in this role, all you can really do is:

1. Make bullying a talked about subject, encourage open conversation, be an active listener and stay child-centred. Empower the child you are responsible for as much as you can.

2. Try your hardest to 'bully proof' the child you are working with. What I mean by this is that you should seek to increase their self-esteem, give them skills to deal with conflict, support and increase their friendships, and ensure that they have a number of safe adults in their life.

3. Ensure that links with the other adults who provide a service or care to the child are strong – good team work where information is shared and where children receive consistent messages are always protective factors.

4. Remember both the bullied child and the bullying child often have similar vulnerabilities and helping/supporting both usually leads to better outcomes.

Activity: Group Dynamic Picture
Purpose

- To give children the opportunity to show you the dynamics in a group and to talk about their position in the group.

What you will need

- large (A2) piece of paper

- pens

- small pieces of paper

- Blu-tack™

- book covering (optional) to cover your big picture to preserve it.

What to do

1. In preparation, draw onto the large piece of paper a scene that has various focal points or places where people would/could join together. You want this to be a place that reflects the child's interests. For example, if the child likes the beach, draw a beach scene with focal points including an ice cream van, a kite, several buckets and spades, and a dinghy in the water. Alternatives might be a play park, school playground, ice rink, club, etc. If you prefer, you could find a picture and enlarge it.

2. With the child, using the smaller pieces of paper and pens, invite them to draw a picture of all the people in the group who you want to discuss. Depending on the child's preference, these could be stick figures with names attached, or elaborate detailed drawings. Try to encourage the latter and, as they draw the other children, ask them to describe them, in terms of both their appearance and their personality traits. This gives you the opportunity to begin to find out about the child's view of the other children. Depending on the number in the group, this might be all you get done in the first session.

3. The next step is to invite the child to place themselves on the picture and then, in their own time, place the other children. Who would they have beside them? Is that the person who they normally play with or the person who they would like to play with? What does it feel like to be there? Is that where they would want to be? What would happen if they moved to this place on the picture, beside this child or in that group? What do they think they would need to do to be able to spend time with the other child or to be on a different place on the picture? How would it feel to be there? What can the helping adult do to support them to join that group?

PRACTICE EXAMPLE

Jane was 6¾. The ¾ was very important to her! She advised me that she had no friends and that everybody hated her. This, to be fair, was not far from the truth, according to her teacher. The teacher reported that Jane regularly pulled people's hair, took the other children's snacks and was rough in her play. She had been called a bully but also reported herself as being bullied. She stated that the other children called her names and would not play with her. We had tried a buddy system but nobody managed to sustain being Jane's buddy.

I began by observing Jane at playtime — it was heart-breaking to watch as she constantly approached other children trying to join in, only to be actively pushed away or ignored. Jane would then resort to pulling hair and running away a little — inviting the other child therefore to chase her. Sometimes this worked, but often the group of girls would react by name calling, and Jane would walk away with her head down and upset.

In my next session with Jane, I produced a picture that I had drawn of the school playground. Jane loved the fact that it was her playground that I had drawn, including the fact that I had drawn in the special bins that the school had and the big tree in the middle of the playground. The fact that I had drawn/made it for Jane was very important to her. Jane put much effort into drawing representations of all her class-mates and was excited to come the next week to play with them on the picture. Through this, we established whom Jane wanted to be friends with. When I took a turn at placing the people on the picture and playing out the scene that I had observed, this increased Jane's self-awareness. Jane said of the hair pulling that she didn't want to hurt them but just wanted to play. We were able to discuss how the girls didn't like having their hair pulled and Jane conceded that she would make them 'sorry' cards, which we did together. I was aware that by removing this way of trying to engage her peers, I needed to give her something else. I agreed with the head teacher that Jane could be given a big bucket of water, some paint pots and old brushes at the next playtime, and that she would be in charge of this water painting activity with the help of the playground assistant. This gave Jane the chance to gain peers' attention.

Together, Jane and I worked out other things that she could do at playtime that might make the other children interested and want to play. This included making houses on the field by placing stones in the shape of a house, making a big spider's web in the tree with wool and taking several bottles of bubble mixture to share. With support, Jane learnt to try and draw people to her rather than trying to push her way into their groups.

Team work was important here. The playground assistants supported opportunities in the playground, and I worked with Jane individually, helping her to think of activities and increasing her self-awareness through the group dynamics picture. Jane's teacher further supported this work by giving Jane jobs to do that meant that she had structured interactions with peers; for example, giving the milk out at playtime. Jane's granny (who was her relative carer) made a point of linking in with a few of the parents of Jane's peers, setting up tea visits and playdates. Two terms later I was pleased to learn that Jane had two good friends and was no longer feeling that she was being bullied.

Activity: Safety Shields
Purpose

- To help a child to develop an internal coping mechanism when faced with an upsetting situation.

What you will need

- a story that illustrates the use of shields (I use *I Fought at Bannockburn* (Ross 2001). For some children, the text is too long and complex, but the important part is the pictures that illustrate the use of shields.)

- a flat piece of cardboard – a shop will usually be happy to give away old packaging

- scissors

- a roll of tin foil

- a glue stick

- A4 white paper

- good quality colouring pens.

What to do

1. Look at the book with the child and talk about how the people are using their shields. Reflect on how strong the shields must be, and explore how the people behind the shields might be feeling. Look together at the pictures of the shields and discuss their purpose.

2. Lead the conversation on to when the child might find a shield handy to have. Children will usually talk about fights and think in a concrete way. You will need to introduce the idea of a shield that could protect your emotions. Your conversation with the child might run like this:

    Child: I could use it to fight with.

    Adult: Yes, you could, just like in the story. What if it were a magic shield that nobody could see but you? Could you hold it up to protect you?

    Child: That would be so cool!

    Adult: Yes, it would be cool because then you could use it anywhere to protect you when people said nasty things to you and hurt your feelings. What do you think?

    Child: Mmmm.

    Adult: I know, let's make a magic shield; it will be so cool [said with enthusiasm]!

3. Help the child to draw out a shield shape on the cardboard to fit their size and cut this out. Apply glue and then cover with tin foil.

4. Admire this shield. Hold it up in front of the child. Wonder aloud if it is strong enough. Lead the conversation on to how to make it strong. Talk about a time when someone has said a nasty thing to you and to protect yourself you thought of all the things you liked doing and that this made you feel good. Explain that this was you using your magic shield that nobody could see and that it was very strong.

5. Help the child to think about the things in their life that they enjoy or that make them feel good. If possible, help them to think of people whom they trust and feel safe with. Suggest to the child that if you draw these things and stick them on their shield, then this will make it strong.

6. Admire the shield. Be really over the top and use lots of exclamations. This is very important because memory is helped by association with sensory experience, so different sounds and facial expressions associated with different pictures on the shield will help the child to remember the pictures. For example, for one picture you might give them a high five; for another you might say, 'Wow!'; for a third you may clap, and so on.

7. When this is done, play a game where you ask the child to close their eyes and to describe their shield. You might need to help and prompt. Really celebrate all the details they remember (the important thing is that they should feel successful). They don't need to remember them all and, if they are struggling, you should end the game. You might end by stating something like, 'You are so clever – you remembered two of your pictures with no peeking. Wow! It must be a really strong magical shield because there is a picture of it in your head. Now if you practise lots and lots, then that picture will get really strong and your magic shield will start to work. Then when someone says something which upsets you, you can see your magic shield, and it will protect you.'

8. Decide with the child where they are going to pin up their shield to practise remembering it. I often suggest that we pin it up on the wall beside the child's bed, so that they can see it before going to sleep. This is useful if nightmares are an issue.

One of the little girls I work with uses her shield when she wakes up after a nightmare or when she hears her parents arguing when she is in bed.

9. Ask the child if they would like to show their carer their shield and maybe help the carer make their own, or help a sibling make one. I encourage this as it reinforces the process, but it is always the child's decision.

This is my picture about Bulling one girl was Shouting at the other girl. She was telling her to fight - but she didn't want to. It was Lucky because a teacher came along to stop it, she Looked after the girl who didn't want to fight. Bulling makes people feel Sad, angry and Scared somehmes!

Chapter 5

Talking to Children About Domestic Abuse

Sadly, domestic abuse is common. The following statistics show the prevalence rates in the UK.

Scotland

In Scotland, the Scottish Crime and Justice Survey 2014/2015 findings on partner abuse were based on interviews with around 11,500 people living in private households, over the age of 16. The results of these interviews showed that 14.1 per cent of respondents had experienced domestic abuse since the age of 16 (Scottish Government 2016).

England and Wales

For the year ending March 2015, the Crime Survey for England and Wales found that 20.2 per cent of adults aged 16–59 had experienced domestic abuse (Office for National Statistics 2016).

Northern Ireland

According to the Northern Ireland Crime Survey 2015/2016, 15.7 per cent of the 1975 adults interviewed had experienced domestic abuse since the age of 16 (Department of Justice 2017).

Statistics across the UK point to women being more likely to be victims of domestic abuse than men. In Northern Ireland, this amounted to 19.3 per cent of women and 11.5 per cent of men interviewed. Findings were similar in Scotland, with 18.5 per cent of women and 9.2 per cent of men reporting domestic abuse since the age of 16. In England and Wales, 27.11 per cent of women and 13.2 per cent of men stated that they had experienced domestic abuse since the age of 16.

It can be daunting to begin to talk to children about domestic abuse. This is perhaps largely because it is unlikely we will ever know the exact details of what has gone on and what the child has witnessed. Also, it is distressing to think of a child experiencing domestic abuse; to feel afraid around the people, and in the place where you should feel safest, is a terrible thing to happen. But, in essence, when you talk to children about domestic abuse, your focus is really on talking about relationships and emotions. If you keep this in mind, the subject should feel more manageable.

It is important to be aware that children are often told not to talk about domestic abuse. Sometimes this is because parents feel a sense of shame. Sometimes the non-abusing parent will have been fearful for their own and/or the child's safety if the abuser finds out they have talked about the abuse. Sometimes the abusive parent will have threatened the child. However, if the message 'You're not to tell' has been conveyed, you can be sure this will have been done with a lot of emotion. The child will take a lot of convincing that it is now okay to talk about the abuse.

It can be extremely helpful (and arguably essential) to the child to work in partnership with the non-abusing parent. That is not to say that the child should not have an opportunity to talk about domestic abuse privately with a worker, but just that there are benefits to partnership working as well. A combination of both approaches is sensible.

- The child needs permission from the non-abusing parent to talk about the abuse.

- The child needs the non-abusing parent to validate their experience.

- The child needs the non-abusive parent to reassure, and give concrete examples of what will be different now/how the child will be kept safe.

Before working with the child, meet with the non-abusive parent. It is not uncommon for a parent to resist the idea that there needs to be a conversation with the child about the domestic abuse, especially if they feel that the child should not know what has happened as 'they were in their room'. It is understandable that there is resistance. Acknowledging abuse has taken place is a huge step. In addition, if you have tried to protect your children by sending them to their room or by managing your abusive partner's behaviour until the child is in bed, then that all may seem pointless if you are now going to talk about it. There is also often a fear of 'opening up old wounds'. However, if the child was in the home when the abuse happened it would be very surprising if they had not had a sense of it having happened. But perhaps the most emotive reason to resist talking to a child about domestic abuse is that in doing this as a parent you are acknowledging that it has had an impact on your child. Most parents feel distressed at that thought and some may feel guilt at having been unable to protect their child(ren).

PRACTICE EXAMPLE

Tammy was convinced that Nathan, aged 4, had no idea about the domestic abuse – she advised that he was always asleep. When her partner hit her, he tended to hit her face and then go to the shop to buy her make-up, insisting that she put this on to cover bruises up.

Just after I was allocated the case, and as part of the social work intervention, Nathan's dad moved out of the home. I initially worked with Tammy and Nathan together, but then offered Nathan some sessions on his own. Initially these were free play sessions. The play opportunities I offered encouraged talk about families. Nathan, whilst using a doll's house, stated to me 'Mummy's not got new make-up now.' I didn't know at that time about his dad's habit of buying make-up to cover up the injuries. However, I judged by the way Nathan had said this that it was of significance. I therefore replied, 'Oh that's interesting, can you tell me more about that?' Nathan replied, 'Yeah, daddy doesn't hit her no more so she doesn't need make-up to make the sore bit disappear.'

If the parent is willing, I will do the same session with them and their child together. Something as simple as providing really nice pens and big pieces of paper, and inviting the parent and child to draw a picture of them as a family can provide the opportunity to talk about domestic abuse, as the below pictures produced by John, age 7, show.

PRACTICE EXAMPLE

When I first became John's social worker, I met with him each week in school for around 30–40 minutes, offering free play. This allowed him to build a relationship with me, and for me to be able to assess John. John had been told 'not to tell' by both of his parents, and this in itself had caused him a great deal of stress. Because I had developed a good relationship with John, he had been able after a few weeks to tell me that he was 'not allowed to talk about home, it's private'. When he said this, I did not then try to press him into telling me why or to talk about home. Instead I reflected his statement back: 'I understand you're not allowed to talk about home because it is private. I wonder can you show me how that feels?' At this I produced some simple cards depicting faces with emotions. I invited John to choose as many as he needed. He picked 'angry' and 'sad'. We talked about the feelings in terms of how they affected him. I did this by drawing round his body as he lay on the floor and then inviting him to show me where the feeling was. For example, he pointed to his tummy when speaking about the 'worried' feeling. We were able to draw what we thought the worry looked like. For John, it was a sleeping monster that was green and made John feel sick. On asking if there was any other part of his body where the 'worried' feeling lived, John pointed to his head telling me, 'I think about "it" all the time. I worry about Mummy…' He then stopped abruptly. I think he was afraid he had said too much. I reassured him that it was okay, that he was just telling me he thinks a lot about his worry.

John nodded vigorously. Having done this with the angry feeling too, and after offering lots of empathy, I suggested to John that Mummy needed to know that the 'not allowed to talk about home because it is private' rule was making him unhappy. I emphasised that he had not broken the rule because he hadn't told me about home, only about his feelings.

John agreed to show Mummy the picture we had made. We agreed to do this together, inviting Mummy to come to our next school session.

A couple of hours before the next session in school I met with John's mum on her own. I explained that I knew about the 'not allowed to talk about home' rule and emphasised that John had not broken the rule, but that he had made a picture to show how this was making him feel. As I predicted, John's mum was defensive and angry. I gave her space to vent these feelings, but once this had settled, I reiterated that John had not broken the rule and that many families had this rule. I wanted to ensure that John's mum knew that I was not criticising or judging her. I explained that I understood the rule would not have been made to deliberately upset or hurt John and that these kinds of rules tend to come about because of fear or shame. However, I explained that it was hurting John a great deal, as it would any child. You will note that I tried to create opportunities to depersonalise this and to impart the message that I had come across this before. I outlined what I would like to happen with positive expectation: 'I know this rule will have been made for really good reasons and I know you have not intended to hurt John. But now it is time to change the rule. That might be quite frightening [pause] but I think you are a strong woman and I hope today you can do this for John.' John's mum got upset and we talked through her feelings and fears. She had left her abusive partner by now, but was afraid that if John talked openly in the community about private family life, then her ex-partner or his family would hear about this and that they may have placed them at risk. We agreed to name the safe adults who John could talk to about anything, including the 'private family' stuff. This included myself as social worker, the teacher and the church minister.

Having worked through this, when John's mum joined me in my session with John, she was able to give John what he needed and react positively to his picture depicting his problem with the 'don't talk' rule. John looked so relieved and went to his mummy for a cuddle. It was a great privilege to be present.

Sometimes finding the words to describe what has happened causes people concern. Some of the common phrases/words I use are 'hurting hands' and 'gentle hands', 'bullying behaviour', 'scary', 'big emotions' and 'shouting part'.

Holly Van Gulden's language of parts (Van Gulden and Vick 2005) is very useful when talking to children about domestic abuse. She takes the idea that we are all made up of many parts, both positive and negative. We have loving parts, sad parts, kind parts, hitting parts, etc., and these parts can work in different ways. This allows for recognition that nobody is all bad. I sometimes ask the child to draw a picture of themselves and then label different parts. This should include emotions, likes and dislikes, and actions. You can then, either at the same session or another, do one for other members of the family. Doing one of these pictures for the abusive parent is helpful as it gives the child permission to be positive about the abusive parent. Below is an example of what the person might look like when all the parts have been labelled.

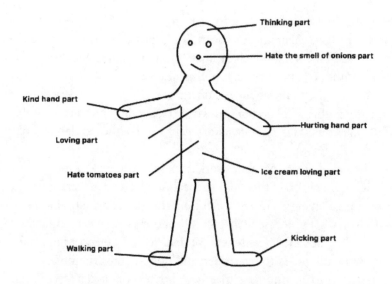

When I did this with John, one of his statements was 'Dad was good fun sometimes. He would lift me way high and I would giggle.' We therefore wrote on the hands, 'lifting way high' parts. John then said that his dad would use 'hurting hands': 'he hurted Mummy lots and me sometimes'.

Because of the way that family life is depicted in our society – through the media and teaching of social norms/ideals – most children will feel that a 'normal family' consists of a mum, dad and the child(ren) living together. Anything other is perceived as different. Children who have lived in a family with both parents, even when they have witnessed domestic abuse, will most likely have a big reaction to the separation of their parents. They will grieve the loss of the family unit and some children may be angry with one or both of the parents. This strengthens the argument for having a conversation about domestic abuse. A lot of children will continue to have contact with the abusive parent. This is often, but not always, supervised. If the abusive parent tries to then pass messages to the non-abusing parent, this can be very distressing for all parties (and arguably this contact should be reviewed). In helping the child to cope with this, I find it helpful to relate this to the child's experiences in terms of peer fall-outs. This can then help a child to understand the dynamic and that it is not their fault. Perhaps the abusive parent is 'behaving like a bully' and 'has forgotten to be friends'. You would then talk about the fact that people can choose to change their behaviour but that they have to want to. Give an example that you know will have meaning for the child. If possible give an example that is true. You may conclude that 'Mummy and Daddy can't be friends right now, but they can both still love you'.

You can then talk about contact if the child is to have contact. Depict how this will happen and when. Depending on the age of the child, you could make a social story cartoon together to depict what contact will look like.

The other focus of your work should be to assess the child's emotional literacy and then aim to increase it. There are simple ways to do this. Playing snap with emotions cards, acting out emotions, using worry activities (see Chapter 11) and making use of children's literature are but a few examples. We believe that the most important thing is a willingness to have open and honest conversations.

It is worth mentioning that it is not uncommon for children who have witnessed domestic abuse to struggle with aspects of relationships. You may note that with adults they are watchful, keen to please and attempt to anticipate what you want. These children can also be described as being exceptionally good, and are sometimes quiet. It is likely that the above behaviour will have stemmed from them attempting to manage the abusive adult – 'If I keep them happy it will be okay.' In domestic abuse, the person whose behaviour is abusive often focuses on a need to be in control. In my experience, children have often either learnt to stay quiet so they do not draw attention to themselves, or perhaps the non-abusive parent has continually coached the child to be quiet, and not disturb or upset the person with abusive behaviour. For these children, using percussion instruments in one-to-one sessions can be helpful. This helps children to learn that in the sessions it is safe to make as much noise as you want. This can be hugely empowering for the child and eventually a lot of fun.

Fun can be sadly lacking in these children's lives. Take every opportunity you get to foster it. The ability to have fun and enjoy the small things in life builds resilience, and none of us can have too much of that!

To get back to a noisy session, a word of advice – tell the school staff if you are likely to be doing this in school, and negotiate which room to use in advance. The last thing you want to happen is to get a child to a place where they are enjoying being noisy and then for a staff member to enter and ask you to keep it down. When I don't have a suitable venue, then I use my car. With the radio on hand and drums and symbols handed out, we park in an empty car park or even a layby, and make all the noise we want!

It is not uncommon for peer relations to be strained for children who have witnessed domestic abuse. Children learn from those around them how to behave in relationships, and parents (or people in a parental role) are usually the ones who have a huge influence. Imagine if one of your heroes in life, the person you have looked up to and wanted to be like, did lots of really good things but, when unhappy with another person's opinion or behaviour, they hit/hurt them. It is only logical that most children in this position will learn to do the same. It is not that they 'have a violent streak in them' (as was once said to me by an ill-informed foster carer) or even that they are 'badly behaved'. It is more the case that they have been taught the wrong way to deal with disputes and the strongest influences in their life have been negative influences in terms of this area of development. This is an important point. I have heard people argue that 'He should know better now – we have conflict resolution' or 'He knows that we do not allow people to hurt each other, we have emotional literacy and friendship skills – there is really no excuse.' Perhaps it is not an excuse but just a fact, that for most children, their parents will be the biggest influence in their lives and they will learn lots from them. If the relationship is healthy the child will, however, feel able to draw on other influences in their lives and the parents will be supportive of this. If you are living in fear (or have lived in fear) you learn how to survive by looking to the strongest and most influential person in the family group (in cases of domestic abuse this will usually be the abuser) and copy their behaviour. You must keep them on side to survive. Even after that influence has changed/ended, it takes a long time to relearn behaviour. Part of this process is finding a new strong influence to model from and being brave enough to let go of previous behaviour that kept you safe. This is true for both adults and children. Take a moment to imagine how hard that is.

EXERCISE

Close your eyes. Remember the most important adult in your childhood. Someone you loved; someone you spent a lot of time with. What did they teach you? Think of something that they always said (e.g. my father taught me to always be on time; he conveyed that not to be on time was disrespectful). Now imagine that someone else, maybe your teacher, told you that this was untrue and the opposite was right. How would that feel? Would it be easy to change your original belief? What lengths would you go to, in order to honour your special person's teaching? For the majority of us this would be hard work and, fortunately, most of us do not live in fear. We can only imagine how much harder it is for a child who has lived in a household of domestic abuse.

Children do relearn but it takes time and care and patience. Open conversations about adults not always being right, separating behaviour from personality, providing positive role models and positively reinforcing desirable behaviour are all good ways to enable change.

PRACTICE EXAMPLE

James was having contact with his two younger siblings and mum. I was supervising the contact at a nursery. Younger sister Gemma grabbed a toy that James had and James responded by hitting her very hard on the head with a plastic brick. Now James's father had hit James's mum on the head frequently in the past. In response to James's behaviour, James's mum intervened. She was very emotionally charged and gave James a very big row. He became upset and began to cry. Mum cuddled Gemma and ignored James, in response to which James stomped off into another area of the playroom. Now angry, he tore down some pictures that other children had made and then kicked a door. Gemma was by now happy and, with no visible injury, she went back to play. James's mum looked at me. I advised that she wait until James was calm and then invite him to talk to her. I advised that she acknowledge that Gemma should not have taken the toy from him but that it was not okay to hurt. I advised that James's mum acknowledge that his dad used to hurt her and kick doors but that he was wrong. I suggested that she talk to James about a different way of sorting out problems. James's mum did this with him. James listened and asked, 'Why did Dad keep doing it?' At this, James's mum looked at me so I suggested that, 'Maybe nobody taught him how wrong it was and how to sort things out in different ways.' I went on to say, 'I bet you can learn from your mum James. I bet your mum can teach you different ways.' James replied that both myself and his teacher didn't like 'hurting hands'. I agreed and noted that his male foster carer, the janitor and his football coach also didn't like hurting hands. These were all male role models to James. James agreed that this was the case.

We then changed the tempo by having a snack. It was time to move on. However, after snack, James asked for pens and paper. He produced a 'sorry' card for Gemma and also a note for the children whose pictures he had damaged (we left this on the nursery wall for them). I praised James profusely for this, as did his mum, and helped him to mend the pictures with tape. I asked (without James's knowledge) the nursery staff if they could write him a note in reply to his 'sorry' letter, which they did:

> Dear James. The children were sad to see their pictures had been ripped. But we understand that sometimes when big emotions happen, we all do things we shouldn't. It was good to get your sorry letter and see you have repaired the pictures – well done! We hope you have a nice time in our playroom this week.

James was very pleased to get the letter. He took it to show and tell at school at my suggestion (I called the teacher to advise her), which created another opportunity to discuss feelings and better ways of dealing with them. The following week in my session with James we made a punching cushion (I brought a white pillowcase and some stuffing, so we only had one seam to sew and some fabric paint pens to decorate it). James brought it to contact to show his mum and thus we continued to reinforce positive ways of dealing with anger.

I would ask readers to note that the above was team work, and a good example of how adults working together can be effective in supporting children and creating change.

Activity: In My House
Purpose

- To stimulate discussion around feelings and behaviour and the locations/times when strong emotions are expressed.

What you will need

- card

- pens

- some preparation time – approximately 20 minutes or less.

What to do

1. Preparation: Cut out the shape of a house and divide it into rooms. This should mirror the rooms in a child's own home. For older children, you might want to do more of a floor plan style of drawing. The following are examples:

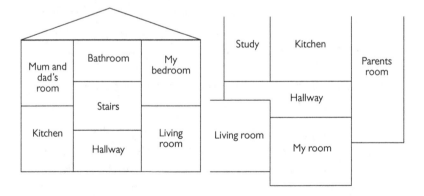

2. Parent's room: You will also need to make a thermometer. Cut it out of card – make it big – A4 size or larger. With the child, decide how you will label it. You will want to mark it in a way that indicates the escalation from calm to cross, to loud, to annoyed, to angry, to furious, to aggressive, to violent.

However, use words that the child suggests. The making of this thermometer is an activity gaining insight into the child's level of emotional literacy and exposure/understanding of others' anger. To elicit the words they want to use, I tend to use lots of acting. I might act out being calm and ask the child what they think I am feeling. I may also use pictures that represent that emotion. Doing this with a sibling group can be easier and a lot of fun because it becomes like a game of charades.

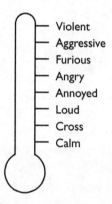

3. Once we have a word of their choice that means 'calm' – a common one is 'chilled' – we write it on the thermometer. I then explain that we need to move up the thermometer a bit and begin to play out being cross. I will ask the child to join in.

4. They will often move to 'angry' and this is okay but I will try to encourage them to think of an emotion before angry. In part this is about me increasing their emotional literacy and perhaps also awareness of the stages of feelings. 'Grumpy' or 'peed off' are common words at this point. Whilst the latter is a bit rude, it has meaning – the child understands it, so personally I just go with it and write it on.

5. We carry on acting and naming – with any child I have worked with I will have already established ground rules in our relationship that I will never hurt them and they are not allowed to hurt themselves or me. As you move towards the aggressive/violent end of the thermometer it is helpful to remind them of this, and have a few cushions to hand that it is okay to hit. You also need to think ahead about an

activity to do once you have completed your thermometer that allows energy/anger to be run off and then settles the child. In other words, we have climbed up the temperature gauge and now we need to cool down! I find ball play outside, followed by a drink and snack and a story (or just chatting if an older child) usually works wonders!

6. Next, make a thermometer that goes from calm to okay, to pleased, to happy, to excited. You will also need a third thermometer that goes from calm to unsure, to scared, to frightened, to terrified. You will also want a spare blank thermometer. So now you have your house and your personalised thermometers.

7. The last thing you need is a pictorial clock that shows key times, detailed in a daily routine. If you have police reports noting when the domestic abuse took place, this can be helpful so that you can be sure to include that key time on your homemade clock (i.e. if the police incident took place when the parent was preparing a meal, you would want a segment in your clock that said 'getting tea ready'). The below is an example of what this might look like.

8. Anecdotally, I would note that points in the day where there is a change/activity (e.g. meal times, mornings when the child is getting out to school) can be key times at which domestic abuse is more likely to occur. The child will often be more in tune with this than the adults. Therefore, whilst you have your clock, have a spare one so that the child can make one too.

9. Draw with the child pictures of their family, including pets.

10. Lay out your house or floor plan, thermometers and your clock. Explain to the child that you want to find out about their family so that you can work out how best to help. Explain that all families are different and everybody has lots of different emotions and behaves in different ways. You are trying to reassure and give the message that there is no right or wrong answer.

11. Ask the child to pick a family member. The choice should include themselves and pets, if any.

12. Ask the child to place the person in the room they think they like best or are in most often. Later, you can ask them to choose the room they don't like/like least. Then, using the clock, ask the child to spin the hand or to choose what time of day it is. Then ask the child to use the thermometers to explain how that person was feeling when they were in that room – yesterday, today or a time they remember well.

An alternative way to use this is for the child to choose the person they want to talk about, use the thermometer to first ask them to indicate which emotion they want to talk about, then place the person in a room and, finally, pick the time of day on the clocks.

On occasions, when children have not been forthcoming, they may have been given very strong messages not to talk about their family or home life, or just not to talk to you! I have used the above at such times to describe what I know has happened. I will only do this when I have a police report that clearly says the child was present so I am not giving them new information.

An example is as follows: 'So the police officer who came to your house wrote me a true story about what happened. I am going to tell you that story and if you can help me with it that would be really good. Because the police officer just knows a little bit. When the police officer arrived, Dad had hit Mum. So I think Dad had been here [indicate 'violent'] on the thermometer but was now about here [indicate 'angry'] when the police arrived. What do you think? You know Dad best. Where do you think he was on the thermometer when the police officer came? Where do you think Dad was before/after the police officer left? Okay, so the police officer said everybody was in the kitchen [place all the people in the kitchen] when they arrived. Yes? Can you show me where everybody was before the police officer arrived? Can you show me with the thermometer what you think people were feeling? Do we need to make another thermometer with different feelings?'

Carry on with the above. Remain curious, be patient and relaxed, ask open-ended questions and be careful not the rush the child. If you do, you become an unsafe adult. If they don't want to participate, just accept this and tell them the story as you know it. Give clear messages of empathy and assurance that none of this was their fault. If you get the above right, you are affirming their position and putting in building blocks to begin to form or strengthen your relationship. By telling them the story as you know it, you are giving them the message that it is okay to talk about it. It also creates opportunities to convey key messages by using affirming statements such as, 'It is never okay for people to use hurting hands', 'It is the police's job to keep people safe' and 'You did the right thing.'

In situations where there is domestic abuse, you need to give the child hope that you and others can help. Telling a child what you will do regarding even small things like getting a panic alarm for the home will help them. Ask the child what they think would help – children can be very insightful. I suggested to a child I worked with that they could stay with their granny at weekends. The domestic abuse to date had happened on a Friday and Saturday when their dad came back from working away from home. I asked if he thought that this would help. He advised, 'Well, so/so.' I asked him if he could tell me more. Taking the thermometer, he said that if he went to Granny's, then he would be 'here' [pointing to 'happy']. He said that Mum would still be at home, and pointed on the thermometer to 'terrified'. I acknowledged but advised that Mum had said that she didn't want to go to Granny's. The child responded by saying, 'Well, maybe you could just buy Mum black bags.' When I questioned this, he said that, 'Dad gets angry when the rubbish is not in black bags, and Mum forgets to buy them.' He placed the figures of Mum and Dad in the kitchen, put the thermometer to 'violent' and used the clock to indicate that it was tea time. This was when his dad returned home.

We arranged for him to go and stay at Granny's and, to help him feel better, we bought a pack of 100 black bags together. He took them home to Mum. This provided him with some comfort, and allowed him to feel okay about staying with his granny.

PRACTICE EXAMPLE

Kerry was 6 years old. She lived with her mum, dad and three siblings. Neighbours reported adults arguing within the home to the police. There had been numerous police reports. Police noted that Mum had sustained bruising; she reported that this was accidental. The children's physical care was poor. They presented as watchful and sometimes withdrawn. Kerry was notably frightened of loud noises and very wary of adults. Clearly something was amiss.

As part of my assessment I arranged to meet all the children individually on a regular basis. Essentially, during these initial sessions I offered free play. The aim was to assess the children's development and build relationships. At a later date, alongside the free play, I would offer some directed play activities (see *Direct Work with Vulnerable Children* by Audrey Tait and Helen Wosu) that would offer opportunities for the child to talk more in depth about themselves and their circumstances. In one of my initial sessions with Kerry, I brought some story books – as one of the choices she could have in her free play. The books were chosen carefully; I had selected stories that were all about families and that had an animal in them, as Kerry loved animals. All the books were picture books and so easily accessible. Reading to children is a good way to build a relationship. It offers the opportunity for close proximity and is a nurturing activity.

Having used the playdough and pens, Kerry chose a story. Her second story choice was *Mog on Fox Night* (Kerr, 2004). In this story, at one point, the dad gets angry when the cat refuses food. At this point in the story I paused and reflected, 'I suppose that's what happens in most families. Kerry – daddies and mummies get angry sometimes but I bet that little cat Mog got a scary feeling in her tummy.' At this Kerry nodded vigorously and stated, 'Me too.' I nodded in agreement but then quite deliberately carried on reading the story. It was tempting at that point to ask more questions, but experience told me not to as this was the first time that Kerry had in any way shared any emotion about family life. It was important not to rush her. Children are very good at dipping in and out of conversations, especially if it is a stressful subject. Respecting and mirroring this can truly aid your communication with them, and support them to talk to you. The other reason I did not ask further questions was simply that it would have disrupted our story. Having a story read to you is a safe and nurturing experience. I was aware that Kerry expected me to continue reading to her. This expectation in itself might have allowed her to begin to share her emotions because she knew that in a minute I would begin to read again. Even if this were not the case, had I begun to explore her experiences mid-story it would perhaps have made storytelling/reading together an 'unsafe' activity from Kerry's point of view.

However, once we had completed the story, we went back through the book, not reading it this time but looking at the pictures and remembering our favourite bits. When it came to the part where the daddy was angry, Kerry stated, 'Oh, this is the scary bit.' I agreed and then asked, 'Do you ever have scary feelings?' Kerry nodded. I empathised and then asked, 'Does your daddy get angry sometimes?' Kerry nodded again. 'Oh dear', I said. 'I guess most daddies get angry. Can you tell me more about when your daddy gets angry?' You will note I normalised the experience/emotion and so remained non-judgemental. My question was said with curiosity. Kerry replied, 'He hits Mummy hard and he hurts me too.' I empathised and continued to ask questions in a gentle manner. During this I started to play with the playdough – just squeezing it in my hands (not modelling it or giving it any attention). I offered Kerry some too, which she took. I did this as I had noted her pulling her sleeve and beginning to pick at the skin on her hand. Through the playdough I was offering her a way to physically express her stress without hurting herself. Kerry described ongoing domestic abuse, as well as abuse of herself and her siblings.

PRACTICE EXAMPLE

Bella, aged 8, lived with her mum. There was a court order which stated that her stepdad would have no contact with either her mum or her, as a result of domestic abuse.

Bella presented well in school, trying hard at her school work. She was popular with staff and children. It was noted that she needed firm boundaries and, if frustrated or if things were perhaps not going her way, Bella could be rough with other children, hitting out to hurt them.

I met with Bella on a weekly basis for about 45 minutes in a small playroom in school.

The sessions had a number of purposes. They were an opportunity to assess Bella's well-being, an opportunity to build a relationship and, most importantly, an opportunity to give her a 45-minute slot in her week in which she had 100 per cent of an adult's attention. She was in charge of what she did in the session, with the only rule being that she was not allowed to hurt herself or me. For a child (or indeed an adult) to regularly have a caring person whose sole focus is them, within an environment where they can lead the interaction, is therapeutic and beneficial in itself. Bella valued her sessions; she remembered when they were and would remind her teacher.

In her initial sessions, Bella explored the whole playroom using all the resources, directing me in great detail about what I was to do. As the weeks progressed however, a theme to her play emerged: that of hiding. We had dinosaurs hiding in bricks, dolls hiding in sandcastles and she would hide the puppets and ask me to find them. Playing hide and seek became a regular game that we *had* to play.

It was unclear to me why this was a theme. I knew that her stepdad had previously hidden from the police when they entered the home. Bella was present and had seen her stepdad arrested, and I wondered if she was processing this. I also wondered if Bella's stepdad was currently breaching his bail conditions and hiding in the home when I visited. I therefore made some unannounced visits and asked the police to do some welfare checks later in the evening. On no occasion did we find her stepdad there or see signs of him being there.

However, a short while later, her mum fled the home with Bella. Bella had been told repeatedly by her stepdad and mum that she was not allowed to tell me. Her mother had, however, now told me and the family were safe.

In the next session with Bella we played, and were about halfway through the time when I noted that the hiding games would usually have begun. So I gently stated in a very quiet voice, 'No hiding games today?' Bella looked at me with full eye contact and said, 'Don't need to now, cause we got a safe home now.' I affirmed that she was living with Mum in a safe place. I remained quiet, and Bella offered, 'He was good at hiding. He was always hiding. Nobody found him.' I replied, 'Yes, your stepdad was good at hiding. Bella I am sorry I didn't find him.' Bella said, 'It's okay, I know you tried hard, I'm sorry I couldn't tell you. He said that I was not to talk to you and Mum did too.' Bella then began to cry and I was able to comfort her.

We made a plan about what to do if this situation arose again. We agreed she could tell her teacher or her gran and then ask them to tell me.

The importance of meeting with her was that, through offering Bella a regular session of play, we developed a relationship where she had felt safe enough to try and tell me about the domestic abuse. It was sad that I had been unable to help effectively at the time, but because I had a relationship with this child we were able to have an honest conversation about this and she, I believe, felt supported.

Chapter 6

Talking to Children About Divorce and Separation

Children may be familiar with the concept of divorce and separation through peers and/or through media. However, adults should not underestimate the impact that divorce or separation can have on a child when it occurs within their own family.

As with other issues within the family, children will probably have been aware that things at home have been difficult, whether consciously or at an unconscious level. Thus, explanations should acknowledge how things have been in the lead up to the decision for a couple to divorce or separate. In doing this, you help to give words to a child's experiences, which will in turn help the child to process both the experience and feelings associated with it.

It is particularly important when talking to children about divorce and separation that they understand that they are not to blame for this. It is not uncommon for parents to have argued over something related to a child, whether that is around the child's behaviour, or negotiating what a child is allowed or is not allowed to do. The adults may quickly forget this, as it is likely to be a small matter in the context of more significant issues at the heart of the relationship breakdown. Children tend to remember such disagreements and blame themselves for the argument. This can then be generalised by the child so that they see themselves as the reason for their parents separating. As such, attention to this is essential and may need to be repeated regularly.

Leading on from this is the need for the child to have an explanation for the divorce or separation. Whether a parent, an extended family member or a professional, it is helpful if you can provide the child with an explanation that both parents are in agreement with. Difficulties arise where one parent provides one explanation, and another parent provides another. This is confusing for the child, and puts pressure on the child to accept one account over another. Clearly, coming to an agreement may be difficult when parents are struggling to be civil to each other, and at such times a neutral third party may be able to communicate with both parents over the matter.

Make sure you choose a venue where you have privacy and where it is okay if the child becomes upset or distressed. Give the child opportunity to ask questions, and, as much as possible, come prepared to reassure the child about the practical consequences of parental divorce or separation.

Typical questions would include:

- Where am I going to live most of the time/some of the time?

- Are we going to have to move house? Where is the other parent going to live/who with?

- Will I be able to go to the same school?

- Will I be able to see my friends still?

- What happens at birthdays and at Christmas (or other significant festivals)?

- Will we still go on holiday?

- Where will my toys be?

- Will I still live with [name of sibling(s)]?

- Why can't we all just still live together?

- Why can't Mummy and Daddy be friends again?

- Who will do [name of task]? (This could include who puts them to bed at night, who cooks them a meal and who does homework with them.)

Even if the child does not ask these questions, you need to offer some explanation so that they can make sense of what the arrangements will be. For younger children, you might draw a picture of two houses, and show who will be in each one. If there are going to be different arrangements in different houses, you might support the parent and child to draw up a list of rules and arrangements for each house so that the child knows what will happen, and where. It is not uncommon for children to experience very different rules and boundaries in place in moving from one parent to another. Where possible, keep the rules and expectations roughly the same. If a parent sees a child less frequently than the other parent, they may struggle to put in place boundaries for fear that the child will then not want to visit them. However, children need stability and boundaries in order to feel safe, and therefore they remain important.

Impact of divorce and separation

Sadly, it is not uncommon for children to feel caught in the middle when parents divorce or separate. Children may hear one parent criticising the other, either because the parent deliberately says this to the child or because they overhear adult conversation. Children are also used at times as a pawn in the relationship, and I have experienced the negative impact on children when parents make allegations against the other in order to gain residence of the child. At such times, children have been asked to tell lies about the other parent or are emotionally blackmailed into saying who they would rather live with. Even when parents do not behave in the ways mentioned above, children can feel their loyalties torn and may worry for the parent whom they are not resident with at the time.

This can be a delicate matter to explain to a child. If you know the child well, you might be able to liken the situation to a time when they fell out with a friend, exploring how they felt. Many children will be able to relate to the feelings of sadness and hurt after such a fall-out. I would explain that sometimes people deal with feeling hurt by not being very nice to the other person and that they may try to make them feel hurt in the same way that they do. There are a number of books that you can use to help tell the story. It is always advisable to read the story yourself before sharing it with the child, to ensure that it is suitable for the child's situation. If working through one of these with a child, you might want to use open questions to explore how the child felt/feels at each stage in the process.

Of course, if you are able to, sit down with the parents individually and help them to understand the impact of this behaviour on their child. If they feel able to, you could support the child to write a letter or poem, or draw a picture, to tell their parents how it feels to be stuck in the middle.

Reconstituted families

Sometimes the child will face the prospect of living with a reconstituted family, whether immediately after a separation or some time afterwards. This can bring its own challenges, and as much as possible this should be done at the child's pace.

Some families can be quite complicated, particularly if all the parental figures have children from a previous relationship. Again, making this visual can be helpful for children and can be used to tell the story.

Some fundamental tips for talking to children about this:

1. Find out what they wish to call the new parental figure. They may wish to call the adult simply by name or refer to them as a 'step-parent'. Children should not be made to call the new parental figure 'Mum' or 'Dad' or any variation on this. Use whatever terms the child uses when speaking about this person.

2. Ensure the child has time and space to ask questions. These might include:

   a) whether they will still get time with their parent by themselves

   b) whether that parent will still want to have time with them and love them as much

   c) whether they will still be able to do old activities

   d) whether their parent and new partner will have a baby together and what this means for them.

3. Include the parent where suitable to offer reassurance to the child about these things.

4. Where possible, reassure the child that the other parent is aware of the new partner, and that they are okay. Children may worry that the other parent will be upset or angry, and

may also need permission to speak about life within the reconstituted family to the other parent.

5. Allow the child to grieve the loss of their old family unit but also try to create a hopefulness about the new family unit(s). The child needs permission to enjoy being part of the new family unit.

6. It is good to try and celebrate both homes' positives especially if the child is living part-time between each parent: for example, at Dad's I have a big garden with a great swing; at Mum's I have a park really close by and I love the chute.

PRACTICE EXAMPLE

Diane was 8 years old. Her mum and dad had separated a week previously, and money problems had been a significant factor in this. Diane had been aware of her parents arguing and had also experienced her dad throwing a glass of whisky over her mum on one occasion. Diane's mum had told her that she was leaving, but hadn't done this in a particularly supportive way. Diane was upset but, at the same time, was glad that the arguments had stopped.

I met with Diane, who told me about what had happened. Diane wasn't sure what was going to be happening, and hadn't been to stay with her mum since her mum left. In fact, Diane didn't even know where her mum was living and she worried that her mum would be sad and alone. I offered Diane some reassurance but had little detail at this time in order to be able to support her.

After some initial work with Diane's parents, I had a number of sessions with Diane. The priority for Diane was to see where her mum was living, so in the first session I took Diane to see her mum's flat. Mum was able to reassure Diane that she was happy where she was, but that at that time Diane couldn't stay with her as there wasn't space.

Subsequent sessions explored the following:

- Through the 'Worries Box' activity (Chapter 11), I established that Diane was worried that she was to blame. Diane had asked for an expensive gift a couple of weeks before her parents separated. As a result of adult conversation and comments made to Diane by her parents when angry, Diane knew that financial difficulties were part of the issue. She worried that she had caused the break up because she had asked for something expensive and it had put too much pressure on her parents.

- Who would look after Diane, once her mum had suitable housing for Diane to stay in? Diane wanted to see both her parents, and they were respectful of this. Diane started to spend a week with each parent. Diane needed reassurance, however, that her parents would do the job of both 'Mum' and 'Dad' when she was living with them. This meant that Dad would cook meals for Diane when she was with him (previously Mum's role) and that Mum would do the bedtime stories (with all the accompanying voices that Dad had done) when she was with Mum. We also explored how Diane would get to school when she lived with Mum, and who would look after her when Mum or Dad were at work.

- Six months after the separation, Dad announced that his new partner Kay was going to be moving in, together with her children. This was difficult for Diane, who I think still had hopes that her mum and dad would get together again in the future. In order to make this more straightforward, a picture was created to explain what was happening. We had three houses – Mum's house, Dad's house and the new partner Kay's house. In Mum's house was a figure of Mum, in Dad's house was a figure of Dad and in Kay's house was a figure of Kay, and her two children, Stacey and John. There was also a figure of Diane. I explained that Kay and her children were going to be moving into Dad's house, and we talked about what this would involve before we moved the figures into the house. Conversation included where the children and Kay would sleep and I explained that sometimes the children would go and visit their dad, and at such times they wouldn't be staying in the house. Using the figures, we acted this out through small world play. We then moved the figure of Diane between her mum's house and her dad's house. Diane could see that sometimes when she was at her dad's house it would just be Dad and Kay, and at other times Kay's children Stacey and John would also be there. After the initial explanation using the figures, Diane played 'families' with the figures. This allowed her to explore this new arrangement in a very practical way, and was something that we could return to as Diane got to know Kay and the children.

Chapter 7

Talking to Children About an Absent Parent

According to the Office for National Statistics (2016), 22 per cent of dependent children are living in lone parent families in the UK. This may be due to divorce, separation, death or because an individual has chosen at the outset to parent alone.

Where children live in a lone parent family, there may be levels of contact with the absent parent or in other cases the child may never have met their birth parent. In the latter case, the lone parent has difficult decisions to make throughout the child's upbringing about what information they provide about the absent parent.

Children grow up in a society in which the norm is that a child will have a father and a mother, and where these adults will be living together and possibly married. As a result, children who are not in this position will start to ask questions from an early age about where the absent parent is. Schools are increasingly aware that the children in their classes may not fit into this norm, whether this is due to living in a lone parent family, with parents of the same sex or because they live with an alternative caregiver, such as foster carers or kinship carers. Despite this, it is likely that the school environment will be the place in which children start to become aware that their family's situation is not like everyone else's, and this can be the time when difficult questions arise.

Before talking to children about an absent parent, there are a number of things that need to be taken into consideration.

1. If you are not the parent of the child, it is important that you establish with that parent what information is going to be

given to the child. Parents and caregivers will (and should!) seek to protect their child from being hurt, and at times this can mean that a child is left without information because of the fear of how that child might respond to information. Where there is resistance to sharing of information, it is helpful to establish what is behind this and see what, if anything, can be done to address this. As is discussed throughout this book, children will seek to fill in the blanks when they don't have information. The child is likely to either romanticise the idea and therefore see this absent parent in an unrealistic light, or, where they have got a sense of this person being negative, their imagination will bring them to consider all sorts of difficult situations.

2. The information given to the child will need to include the reason for that parent being absent. This reason may well be difficult, and the lone parent may struggle themselves to give this information. Reasons may include the absent parent being a perpetrator of domestic abuse, having left the lone parent during pregnancy/after birth with no ongoing contact or being a perpetrator of sexual assault or rape. It may also be that an individual became a parent through the use of an egg or sperm donor. If you are the parent of the child, you may wish to have someone with you for support, and if you are a professional or other adult, you will need to consider whether the lone parent will be present and what support they might need. We would suggest that you work with the lone parent and agree together how you will present the information to the child. Practise the language you will use. Remember that the parent is the expert on their own child, and will know the words that the child would understand. They are also likely to know what will trigger upset. Let the parent lead in this. Only guide as and when required.

3. Whilst it may sound obvious, always remember that the child in question is in part the product of this absent parent. This is significant for a number of reasons. First, the child has a right to know who they are and the absent parent is one part of this identity. Second, if the person in question is absent by choice, children may struggle to understand this and to

come to terms with why a parent has chosen not to see them. If it is the lone parent who has made this decision, the child may also struggle to understand the reasons why. Third, if the person in question has behaved in a way that is abusive or difficult, the child may question their own character and who they are in relation to this person. I worked with a child who had experienced domestic abuse and was aware that his father was not living in the home because of this. The child saw himself as 'bad' based on the fact that he was in part the product of his father, and this was perpetuated by the fact he was male. He believed that he would go on to be abusive to other people, just as his father had been. It is perhaps not surprising that this happens – how frequently we hear phrases such as, 'You're just like your father', often presented in a negative way. In addition, in my experience, I have come across families where there is a belief system which promotes the idea that boys will inevitably become like their fathers and girls like their mothers. This can be very damaging when the lone parent has attributed behaviours to the absent parent (when the same gender as their child) that are undesirable.

Talking to the child

The age and stage of the child will dictate both how much information you give and what preparatory work you need to do with the child, so not all the suggestions below will be suitable for all children.

Younger children will need help to understand that families can look different and are not all the same. Exploring this with a child can be a helpful way of introducing the subject of an absent parent.

Activity: Different Families

Purpose

- To help children understand that not all families look the same.

- To start to introduce the subject of their family's composition.

- To provide children with an opportunity to ask questions about their family.

What you will need

- A3 paper with a circle drawn in the middle and 'roads' going off across the paper. You could draw a street at the top and bottom if you wish and make the circle into a park. Use your imagination!

- Blu-tack™ or glue

- some pictures of children – some can be of one child, and some with more than one child. Include a mixture of ages from babies to adolescence, and be mindful of matters of diversity (you could draw these, choose ready-drawn images or even get the child to draw them)

- some pictures of houses – you could draw these or print them off. You want these to be different sizes and types; you might include a block of flats, a bungalow, large and small houses

- some pictures of different adults – these are to be the types of family, so suggestions include a two-parent family, a single-parent family, a kinship carer (e.g. grandfather), a family where the extended family also live in the house and a reconstituted family (e.g. other children from a previous relationship)

- some pictures of different pets – you could source these yourself or have blank pieces of paper for the child to draw.

What to do

1. Bring out the picture and place the pictures of the children into the middle of the circle. If you are choosing to do so, this is where you would ask the child to help draw some pictures of children.

2. Explain to the child that all these children have been playing together but that it is now time for them to go home. Explain that you need the child's help in order to put all the children in their different homes.

3. Ask the child to choose one of the children from the middle. Bring out the pictures of the different houses and explain that children and their families live in different types of houses and that they are not all the same. Some people live in flats, whilst others live in houses. Some children have big houses,

whereas other children have small houses. Invite the child to choose one of the houses for the picture of the child that they have in their hand, and then ask the child where on the street or road they wish to place this house. You can then either stick the house to the paper with Blu-tack™ or glue it down. Invite the child to place their picture of a child(ren) in front of the house.

4. Next, bring out the pictures of the different adults and explain that, just as children have different houses, so they can live in different types of families. Ask the child to choose which of the different pictures of the adults they are going to choose for their first child and house. Whichever picture they choose, you can either invite the child to think who these people might be, or reflect back. An example would be, 'I see you have chosen a family where there is both a mummy and a daddy – so in this house they are the ones who are looking after the child(ren)?' Depending on the age of the child, you may also wish to ask the child whether they know of any children who have this kind of family.

5. Next, you ask the child if this family is going to have any pets. Let the child either draw a pet of their choice, or choose one of the pictures of pets you have.

6. Repeat steps 3–5 for the rest of the pictures of the children until all the children have houses, adults and pets.

7. At this point, you might ask the child what they think about the different families and which family is most like theirs. You may also ask the child if they have any questions – this may be a time when the child starts to ask about their own family situation. You will want to reiterate that families look different, and not all families have the same people living in them. This can then lead on (either this session or another session) to a discussion about the child's family.

It may also be helpful to explain a parent's absence in the form of a story. This could be one you use through creating a cartoon story or by telling the story orally. Below is an example of what this could look like. Finding colleagues who are good artists is always a bonus!

A LONG TIME AGO, BEFORE YOU WERE BORN, YOUR MUM AND DAD LIVED TOGETHER.

YOUR DAD IS CALLED JOHN. WHEN HE LIVED WITH YOUR MUM, HE HAD BROWN HAIR AND WORE GLASSES. HE WAS AS TALL AS GRANDAD.

YOUR MUM AND DAD WERE BOTH HAPPY WHEN THEY FOUND OUT THEY WERE GOING TO HAVE A BABY

BUT BEFORE YOU WERE BORN, DAD STARTED TO TREAT YOUR MUM BADLY. HE CALLED HER NAMES AND ALSO HIT HER.

MUM WAS VERY SAD AND SHE WAS ALSO SCARED THAT YOU WOULD BE HURT AFTER YOU WERE BORN

MUM MADE A PLAN TO KEEP YOU SAFE. SHE DECIDED NOT TO LIVE WITH DAD ANYMORE. SHE WENT TO LIVE WITH GRANNY AND GRANDAD

DAD WASN'T TOLD WHERE THE HOUSE WAS SO MUM AND YOU WOULD BE SAFE.

IT HAS BEEN MANY YEARS SINCE MUM HAS HEARD FROM HIM.

AFTER YOU WERE BORN, MUM MOVED TO THE HOUSE WHERE YOU NOW LIVE

Children will probably want to know what their absent parent looks like, if they don't already know. A photo, if you can get one, can be helpful but if not then describing what the person looks/looked like is also helpful. When older children don't know what the absent parent looks like and have little information about them, the child may try to find the parent themselves. With social media, this is now much easier to do, and is another reason for giving the child accurate information about the person, even when that information is not positive.

It is likely that the most difficult part of telling the child about the absent parent is where there has been trauma and/or abuse, or where the absent parent has had difficulties (e.g. substance dependency, mental health problems). In such situations, the information needs to be given at an age- and stage-appropriate level, with the focus on the negative aspect as behaviour, not personality. What this means is that you would describe the behaviour as negative, not the person in question. For example, rather than say that the person was a 'bad' man or woman, you would speak of them having done something that was harmful or hurtful. It is important that you do not come across as judgemental of the absent parent, and describing someone as 'bad' may raise questions for the child about whether they are also 'bad', given that they are this person's child. Even when you have been careful in your explanation, you need to be aware that this may be a concern for the child and so it is important to offer reassurance. This is particularly key if the child was conceived as a result of a rape, and in this very difficult circumstance you may need to provide a lot of emotional support to the child (and the lone parent) in coming to terms with this. Once you have given them this information, it is important that you reassure the child that what has happened was not their fault.

For older children and children who have been asking questions, you might start by saying, 'I know that you are/may be wondering about who your mum/dad is, and that you may have lots of questions about them.' You may invite the child to tell you what they already know about the absent parent, or to ask any questions they might have. For a child who is struggling to ask the questions, you could invite them to draw or write them down on sticky notes, or to have a selection of questions and the child choose the ones they want to ask (with space to ask any that you haven't thought of). Having the opportunity to come back to you or their chosen safe adult is important, as the child will probably need time to process what you have told them.

Chapter 8

Talking to Children About Problematic Alcohol Use

Alcohol is a common feature of life in the majority of Western cultures and, increasingly, binge drinking is coming to be seen as a key feature of a night out. However, the fact that alcohol is widely accepted and a cultural norm can be confusing for young people when they then encounter someone with an alcohol problem. It is not against the law to use alcohol as it is with drugs, and it is visible to children and young people in daily life; for example, on sale at the local shop and supermarkets, seen on television both in advertising and in TV shows, and consumed in restaurants and family pubs.

The stereotype of an alcoholic is perhaps the homeless older man who drinks bottles of cheap alcohol by himself. The association with this being a male occupation and something done alone clearly only accounts for some of those who experience problems with alcohol use. In addition, the 'homeless' stereotype presents the idea that this doesn't happen within families.

Children may be reluctant to talk about a parent's alcohol use and may find talking to you about this quite difficult. It is important to recognise the secrecy that can go along with alcoholism, either from the adult themselves and/or as a product of a family 'covering it up'. As a result, talking about this outside the family may feel like a betrayal, through either the implicit or explicit messages that the child has been given. If you are a member of the same family, the child may seek approval from you that it is okay to talk about this.

What is problematic alcohol use?

It is important to understand what a child's lived experience and knowledge of problematic alcohol use is. Again, it is essential that information given is at an age-appropriate level whilst not shying away from helping children to understand the specifics of problematic use. What is key when speaking about problematic alcohol use is, first, the dependency and, second, the impact on both the person using the alcohol and those around them.

Dependency

Older children may be familiar with words such as 'addiction' and 'dependency', but won't necessarily fully understand these terms, so you need to make sure you define this for them in conversation. You may wish to explore both the physical and psychological aspects of addiction. Younger children may need an analogy to help them understand. I (Becky) have found that breaking this down into several steps can be helpful, and you may wish to create a words and pictures story (see Chapter 11), to illustrate this.

1. Some adults choose to have drinks that contain something called alcohol. Alcohol can change the way a person feels and behaves. Some people feel relaxed and some people feel happier when they have had a drink of alcohol.

2. Some people, however, can become aggressive or out of control when they drink, and this can be frightening to be around.

3. A lot of people can drink alcohol and safely enjoy it. However, some people find it hard to stop drinking alcohol. This can be for lots of reasons including because the person likes how they feel when they have had a drink, because they can forget about problems for a while or because it relaxes them. (You may wish to include why the person in question has problems with their alcohol use or ask the child what their understanding is of this.)

4. When alcohol becomes something that a person feels they need, when the person spends time thinking about alcohol or the alcohol use becomes so important that the person needs

to drink before they do other things, then this may mean that the person has a problem with their alcohol use. This can be called 'dependency' or 'addiction'.

Impact – how drinking affects the person and other people

Impact on the person with problematic use

It can be helpful to talk about how alcohol changes a person's character both at the time that they are drinking and afterwards. What is key to this is helping the child to identify what behaviours they see and to think about how they feel when the person is behaving in that way. The activity 'Emotions of Drug Use' (see Chapter 9), can also be used when discussing problematic alcohol use.

Activity: Always, Sometimes, Never

Purpose

- To help the child to understand the impact of alcohol use.

- To help the child to identify how they feel as a result of problematic alcohol use.

What you will need

- a large piece of paper with three headings – Always, Sometimes and Never

- a series of cards with behaviours/feelings written on them

- examples might include: sleeping/being sleepy, being angry, laughing lots, falling over/stumbling, hiding alcohol, sweating, speaking slowly, being sick, being very affectionate

- blank cards and pen for the child to add additional behaviours/feelings.

What to do

1. Having already explored with the child that alcohol can change how people feel and act, explain to the child that

you will be thinking about the person in question who has problematic alcohol use.

2. Explain that there are three headings and, for each word/sentence, you will ask them whether this is a behaviour or feeling they always see when this person has been drinking, sometimes see or never see.

3. Give the child each card, reading it out as you do. When all the cards have been read out you can ask the child if there are other ones they can think of and these can be written on the cards.

4. Whilst doing the exercise you may wish to repeat back what the child is saying, for example, 'I hear you telling me that when x is drinking, they are sometimes sleepy.' This conveys to the child that you are listening and also gives them the chance to correct you if you have misunderstood. At the end ask the child about particular things they have placed down, and which behaviours/feelings are easier or harder to be around. Be gentle in your questions, remaining curious and supportive as you do so.

Impact on others from problematic alcohol use

The activity above starts to explore how others may feel as a result of the behaviours of someone who has problematic alcohol use. The 'What I Need' activity in Chapter 9 may also be useful to look at the impact on the child as a result of problematic alcohol use.

You may wish to think about the key people around both the child and the person with problematic alcohol use, and explain that people are affected in different ways and may respond differently. It is helpful to look at both the emotional and practical ways in which people are impacted.

If you are working with the whole family you might consider doing this activity with a sibling group or the non-alcohol dependent parent and children. This would give a strong message that talking about this problem is okay. You will need to have a good assessment of family relationships and dynamics to judge whether this would be helpful or not.

Depending on the presentation/level of self-awareness of the alcohol dependent person, you may also wish to complete this exercise with them. This could help them to consider the child's lived experience/the impact of their behaviour on the family unit. This would need to be followed up with work to support them emotionally, and to offer the possibility of support for their alcohol dependency.

PRACTICE EXAMPLE

Nicky and Ruth are 12- and 15-year-old sisters. They live at home with their father and stepmother Louise. Nicky had been referred to a voluntary service offering her emotional support in response to her having started to self-harm and miss school. It transpired that this had started in response to her father's increasing alcohol use. Both Nicky's father and Louise dealt with difficulties by ignoring them and the implicit message for the children was that they shouldn't speak about the alcohol use, either amongst themselves or outside the family unit. When Nicky did start to discuss home life in her appointments with the voluntary service, she expressed that she felt helpless seeing her father drink and described a number of emotions including fear, sadness and anger.

During one session Nicky was supported to look at how her father's problematic alcohol use had impacted upon the family as a whole. Prior to this activity, Nicky believed that she was the only family member struggling to deal with this, and this had led to self-blame. It was important to explore the family dynamics so that Nicky could appreciate the impact that her father's drinking had on the family as a whole despite appearances to the contrary.

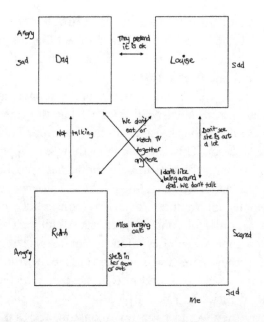

Dad — Angry, Sad

They pretend it is ok

Louise — Sad

We don't eat or watch TV together anymore

Not talking

Don't see she is out a lot

I don't like being around dad. We don't talk

Ruth — Angry

Miss hanging out

She's in her room or out

Scared

Me — Sad

Through this activity, Nicky realised that her stepmother and sister Ruth also struggled with her father's alcohol use, but that they coped with this by isolating themselves or leaving the home, something that Nicky couldn't do as much because of her younger age. Nicky also saw that this had impacted upon her relationship with them as well. Through looking at the family situation as a whole, Nicky was able to recognise that she was angry with her stepmother for not challenging her father about the issue. With this awareness and support to do so, Nicky decided that she would try to speak to her stepmother and sister about the drinking. Nicky and her sister were able to speak to each other, and this brought them both support. Unfortunately, Nicky's stepmother would not speak about the issue in any ongoing way, although Nicky did learn that her stepmother had been encouraging Nicky's father to address his problematic drinking. As a result of an improved relationship between Nicky and her sister, as well as having more understanding of the family situation, Nicky felt less hopeless. Her self-harm decreased over time and she started to attend school again regularly. She continued to have emotional support from the voluntary agency.

Supporting a child affected by problematic alcohol use

As with any substance use, children need to feel that they are able to respond in case of an emergency. A safety plan can be drawn up to help the child know what to do.

Children also need to know that there is support available to someone who has problems with alcohol but that the person in question has to make the choice to do that, and may not admit that they have a problem. This is a common thing to happen and, for people who live with the person with problematic alcohol use, this can be upsetting and frustrating. You might want to talk about this in terms of people not wanting to take responsibility, and through concepts of actions and consequences. Most children will be able to think of a time when they didn't want to take responsibility for something they were doing wrong, perhaps partly because of the shame they would feel, and also because of the consequences. For example, if they had eaten a piece of birthday cake before the birthday party they would get a row (consequence) and the parent would be disappointed in them (leading to shame). They may be asked to go and buy another cake with their money (consequence). It is not surprising that both adults and children sometimes want to avoid dealing with problems, even when the problem is hurting others they love. Exploring this with the child will help develop empathy though of course it does not excuse the adult's unacceptable behaviour (i.e. alcohol dependency). Be sure to emphasise this and remind the child that it is not their fault or their responsibility to stop the problematic alcohol use.

Chapter 9

Talking to Children About Problematic Drug Use

The first myth to dispel is that you have to have an expert knowledge of drug use in order to talk to children about problematic use. However, if you do want to access more information about drugs, there are a number of resources available both online and usually in the community for yourself and/or for the young person.

Things to consider

- *Age of the child* – the developmental age of the child will need to be taken into account in talking to the child about drug use. However, on numerous occasions I have encountered children who were considered by adults to be too young to have a knowledge of a parent's drug use. Frequently these children had much more of an understanding than those around them would believe. One such example was of a 3-year-old boy who took the foil off the display at his nursery and pretended to 'cook' it on a spoon in the home corner, mirroring the behaviour he had seen at home.

- *The identity of the drug user* – the fact that drug use is illegal and stigmatised means that children may have been given either explicit or implicit messages not to speak about it. In addition, the involvement of social services may be a threatened (and real) consequence of problematic drug use being disclosed. As such, children and young people may feel unable to speak about it, particularly when this user is a caregiver such as a parent.

- *Language* – the word 'drugs' can refer to both illegal and legal drugs, to prescription and non-prescription drugs. This can be complicated for children and young people to make sense of. First, drugs can be used as another word for medication and, therefore, children need to understand that some drugs can be bought or prescribed to make people better (e.g. paracetemol, ibuprofen). This is further complicated, however, by the fact that prescription drugs may be abused, and that some drugs have until recently been legal (new psychoactive substances). The chart below demonstrates this, but be mindful that users may take a combination of drugs that cross categories.

Category	Example
Legal non-prescribed drug, then misused	Compound analgesics, e.g. co-codamol, codeine and ibuprofen
Legal prescribed drug, then misused	Gabapentin, diazepam, methadone, valium
Previously legal non-prescribed drug	New psychoactive substances (illegal in the UK since May 2016), e.g. mephedrone, spice, clockwork orange
Illegal drugs	Heroin, cocaine, amphetamines, ecstasy

When talking about legal drugs, whether prescribed or not, the key issue is the misuse of the drug and the impact of this misuse. Areas to cover are as follows.

What is problematic drug use?

- It is important to get an understanding of what the child or young person understands by drug use, so that you can not only build on their existing knowledge, but also correct any misunderstandings that they have. For example, many families I (Becky) have worked with do not consider cannabis a drug. A number of children I worked with thought that 'legal highs' (new psychoactive substances) could not be dangerous because at that time they were legal.

- As with talking to children about any subject, it is important to use plain but accurate language, and help children to understand any terms they might not be familiar with. Below is an example of what you might wish to cover, but this will need to be done at the pace of the child and may involve multiple sessions. For each line, try to make it personal to the individual in question and involve the child or young person wherever possible in contributing to this. Once an explanation has been given, invite the child or young person to ask questions and talk about their experiences. An example of this is in parentheses.

Drugs can come in different forms such as tablets, liquids or powder. ('Do you know anything about the drugs that your dad takes? Tell me about what you know?' – 'The overall name of the drugs that Dad takes are called "legal highs" or "new psychoactive substances" and he takes one called "Benzo Fury". He takes it as a tablet or as a powder.')

Different drugs have different effects on people, for example, they can make people feel happy or relaxed or have lots of energy. ('Tell me about how Dad is when he takes Benzo Fury.' – 'What I know is that when dad takes this drug, he appears to see and hear things that aren't there, and he can have lots of energy and appear very happy. At other times he can be very worried and scared.')

Once the effect has gone, people can feel worse and this is sometimes called a 'come down', a 'crash' or a 'withdrawal'. Sometimes this feels so bad that people then feel that they have to take more drugs to stop feeling this way. ('Tell me about how Dad seems when the drugs have worn off.' – 'What I know is that when Dad is coming off Benzo Fury, he says that he feels very worried, and sad. He also tells me that he gets angry with himself for having taken it and says that he won't use it again.')

Drugs can be physically and/or psychologically addictive, which means that people find it hard to stop taking them once they have started. ('Although Dad wants to stop, he misses the feelings he gets when he does take Benzo Fury. He also remembers all the problems that have happened since he started taking the drugs, and so takes more drugs so that he can forget the problems.')

Drugs are dangerous for a number of reasons. It is not possible to know what the drugs are made with, and when people buy drugs they don't know how strong or weak they are, and so might take too much by accident. When people have taken drugs and are 'under the influence', they might do things that are dangerous because their brain isn't working properly. Drugs can also make the body have to work harder and can put strain on organs such as the heart. Some drugs can also affect the brain so that the brain doesn't work properly even when the person isn't taking drugs. ('People are trying to help your dad because he doesn't recognise what is dangerous or not dangerous when he takes Benzo Fury.')

Why does this person use drugs?

This can be a difficult subject to approach for a number of reasons. Children will frequently see themselves as to blame or contributing towards ongoing misuse. This is particularly the case for young children (around 8 years old and younger), who see the world in relation to themselves, and thus will see themselves as at least partly responsible for events. Children need reassurance that they are not to blame for drug use. A second issue lies in confidentiality. Whilst children may have the right to know about problematic drug use if it is impacting upon their lives, they are unlikely to have the right to know about the reasons behind this. I have found that children who are aware that a parent's drug use was their way of coping with adverse experiences have been able to understand their life story in a fuller and more coherent way.

- Try to find out what the child knows or has been told about why the person uses drugs. If possible, seek to come to an agreement with the person using the drugs about what explanation can be given. However, it is important that the child is told the truth. It may be tempting to give a more sanitised or positive version, but this undermines a child's ability to trust you when they find out the truth at a later stage. Be aware that there are likely to be several factors at play.

- Reasons for initial use/continued use may include to relieve physical pain, to escape from emotional pain, as self-medication for mental health problems, in response to peer pressure, not appreciating the dangers of use and addiction, boredom or to have lots of energy or feel 'high'.

- When providing an explanation, it is important not to be critical or judgemental of the person who has problematic drug use as this is likely to lead a child to be defensive of the person in question. However, it is also important that the child understands the negative consequences of drug use, and why it is not a safe or healthy solution.

PRACTICE EXAMPLE

Sally came into foster care at 9 years old, as a result of her father's problematic drug use. Sally presented as angry with her father, but also blamed herself, aware that her dishevelled presentation at school and low attendance had been one of the early indicators to professionals that there were concerns about her care.

Sally initially spoke to no one but, over time, started to talk to her foster carer about her experiences. Whilst her foster carer felt ill-equipped to answer some of Sally's questions, Sally refused to speak to anyone else about life at home.

One of the questions that Sally kept asking was why her father had not stopped using drugs when he was aware that the alternative was that Sally would be taken out of his care. She believed that she was not good enough, and that he did not love her enough.

The foster carer told Sally a story – whilst it will not be suitable for young children who may find the analogy confusing, it really helped Sally to understand more about what 'addiction' is. She did this by talking about chocolate! The following is a modified version of the story that Sally was told:

A long time ago, your father Peter took some drugs for the first time – and it was a bit like eating the most amazing chocolate in the world. Imagine that this was the tastiest 'chocolate' in the world but also was magic, and helped him to forget about all the worries that he had.

The problem was that a few hours after Peter had this 'chocolate' he started to feel really bad. He didn't feel very well and all the worries came back. In fact, the worries felt worse than they had before he had the 'chocolate'. So what he did was get some more 'chocolate', and then he started to feel good again.

Soon Peter was having 'chocolate' a lot of the time, because every time he stopped eating it, he felt bad again, so he had some more, and on and on it went.

Peter knew that the 'chocolate' wasn't good for him, and people told him he should stop having it. He also knew that he might not be able to care for you and live with you if he didn't stop. So he tried to stop, on a number of occasions. But the tastiest 'chocolate' in the world was very hard to stop taking. When he didn't have the 'chocolate' he remembered how bad things had got since taking the 'chocolate'. So, although it was the 'chocolate' that had caused the problems, it also made him forget the problems. Also, Peter's body was now used to having 'chocolate' and when he didn't have it, he felt unwell. It was so hard to say no to the 'chocolate' when it was the only thing that for a while made him feel better in both his mind and body.

The foster carer then spoke to Sally about who was working with her father, in order to try and help him to recover from his substance misuse. As Sally got older she became more aware of the difficult experiences that her father had had in the past. This then helped her to understand more of why her father sought to 'escape' through drugs.

What is the impact of problematic drug use?

When thinking about the impact of problematic drug use, you may want to consider both the practical and emotional impacts of the use. Children who have lived/are living with someone with problematic drug use will have a lived experience and will have developed their own understanding of this in line with their developmental stage and (limited) life experience. They may, however, have misinterpreted experiences, and so will benefit from the opportunity to explore their experiences and to gain a better understanding.

How you talk about this to a child will depend on their ability to speak openly about any experiences they have of living with or having contact with someone with problematic drug use. Children who don't have the lived experience or who struggle to be open about their experiences will benefit from a more 'generic' exploration of the impact of problematic drug use. Those who can speak openly will be able to explore this in terms of their own experience.

The below activities can be quite powerful, so it is important that care is taken to ensure that the child is supported both during the exercise and afterwards. You may wish to come up with a special word that the child will say if they want to stop the activity at any time.

Activity: What I Need (or 'What Children Need' if keeping it generic)

Purpose

- To help children understand what they need from those around them and how this can be impacted by problematic drug use (when this is a caregiver).

What you will need

- a large piece of paper with 'What I Need' written on it

- a large of piece of paper split in two, with 'Always' written on one side and 'Never' written on the other

- small pieces of paper or card (approximately 10 cm square)

- pen(s).

What to do

1. Explain to the child that you are going to think about all the things that a child needs from the adults around them and how this can be affected when someone uses drugs.

   Either:

   a) Ask them to come up with ideas for what children need, for example food, a house, encouragement. The child and/or you then draws an image or writes a word to represent this. Keep a list of what you want to cover (see point b) and suggest these if they are not mentioned by the child. Each completed paper should be placed on the large piece of paper entitled 'What I Need'.

   b) Bring with you pre-drawn/printed images and 'deal' them out to each person taking part, including yourself. Each person then takes a turn putting their card on the large piece of paper entitled 'What I Need' and has to guess what the image means. The following is a suggestion of what you might want to include, but also have some blank pieces of paper so that the child can draw/write additional ideas. List: Food and drink, a safe place to live (i.e. a flat or house), a clean environment, toys, to be able to be clean and have clean clothes, friends, to be able to go to school, enough money, being able to go to medical appointments, adults who keep me safe, someone to teach me right and wrong, encouragement and praise, being safe, quality time with family, play, a chance to go to clubs and groups, love, cuddles and hugs.

2. Gather up each small piece of paper with the images on them. Speak to the child about how someone who takes drugs may not always be able to care for a child as that child needs. One at a time, take each piece of paper and ask the child whether they think that they always, sometimes or never get what they need from the substance-using parent. The child will then place the piece of paper under 'Always' or 'Never', according to their answer. You might also want to have a middle section called 'Sometimes'. If doing this generically,

you would need to ask about whether drugs stop someone giving a child…[name the need] always, sometimes or never. An example might be going to school. Mum is able to get me to school always, sometimes or never.

3. For children of a younger developmental stage, you might use the headings 'This is okay – no problem' and 'They can't do it'. You could draw thumbs up and thumbs down symbols to go with these headings. You may also need to help the child to decide, if they have lived with consistent drug use for a long time. This is because they may well accept even a pretty minimal level of care as normal and not have anything to compare their experiences against. They may also not recognise that it is the drug use that prevents the adult from supporting them, so you may need to guide them; for example, 'I find your mum sleeps more than most adults I know, which is because of the drugs. When she is asleep she can't…'

4. When finished, it can be helpful to explore what the child has put down in each column. It may also help the child to understand why certain decisions have been made with regard to them because of the problematic drug use. You may also be able to have a discussion with the child about how some of those areas affected can be supported.

PRACTICE EXAMPLE

Maddie is a 10-year-old girl who came into foster care as a result of neglect by her parents. This neglect was predominantly caused by parental substance misuse. Maddie was aware that her parents misused substances and was also aware that her needs were not fully met at home.

Maddie had been in foster care for a number of years and, whilst she did not want to return home, she still blamed herself for the initial accommodation. The catalyst for Maddie coming into foster care was that she had been found by a stranger a long distance from her home at a young age. Maddie had believed that this was her fault for having wandered away from the home. As her social worker, I had spent a number of occasions discussing this with Maddie, and her foster carers had done the same.

During life story work with Maddie, I used the exercise 'What I Need'. We initially went through all the cards, naming all the things that children need. Maddie was interested and engaged in this process. We discussed how children needed lots of things from the people who looked after them to ensure that they were happy, healthy and safe. I then suggested that we went through the cards again using three pieces of paper. One said 'always', one said 'sometimes' and one said 'never'. This time I asked Maddie to say whether the need identified on the card was something that she 'always', 'sometimes' or 'never' had when in the care of her parents. The card was then placed on the appropriate piece of paper. During this process, Maddie spoke about life at home in an open way, disclosing to me things I had not previously been aware of.

When we came to the end of the exercise, there were many cards on the 'never' piece of paper, with only a few on 'always' or 'sometimes'. I voiced this observation to Maddie, who had gone very quiet and appeared reflective. I said I was sorry that this had been her experience, and that her mum and dad had not been able to give her what she needed. I was also able to help Maddie see that the incident in which she had been unsupervised was only a small part of the wider picture, and that she was not to blame for these things. As a result of this exercise Maddie was able to recognise that she was not to blame for coming into foster care.

Activity: Emotions of Drug Use
Purpose

- To help children understand their emotions and how they are impacted by a significant other's problematic drug use.

What you will need

- a large sheet of paper with a number of emotions drawn out on it. It is possible to buy an emotions chart quite easily, if you don't want to create your own

- a number of cards that have statements on them naming behaviours associated with problematic drug use. You can make these as generic or specific as is helpful for the child in question. You may need several copies of each card.

What to do

1. Explain to the child that the activity is to help explore how it can feel to be around problematic drug use.

2. Look at the emotions chart (ensuring for younger children that they understand what each one means) and explain that we can sometimes have lots of different emotions in response to one thing. Give an example: performing on stage in front of the school might feel worrying, scary and exciting at the same time.

3. Explain that you have a number of cards, each of which describes how someone who has used drugs might behave. Ask them to put each card on the emotions chart to say how they would feel being around this behaviour. Explain that you have spare cards so that they can put a card on more than one emotion.

4. As each card is read out and put down, there is an opportunity to explore this with the child and understand the reason why they have chosen the emotions in question.

5. Once all the cards are laid out, there is an opportunity to reflect on which emotions are most frequently identified. You may want to talk to the child about how it is not unusual to have a lot of different emotions and that these may be difficult emotions to feel. Where a child feels able to talk about it, you can ask them to think about their own experiences and the resulting emotions.

Supporting a child affected by problematic drug use

If a child continues to have contact with, or live with an adult who uses drugs, it is important that they can feel empowered to know what to do in the case of an emergency. Practice this with the child.

Children also need to know that if someone is using drugs, then this doesn't always have to be the case. You can explain that there are people whose job it is to help adults come off drugs, but that sometimes this can take some time, and that the adult who is taking the drugs has to want to do this.

Children may have a lot of questions. You may wish to brainstorm these questions on a piece of paper, or use the 'Worries Box' activity referred to in Chapter 11. If you don't know the answer to their worries, tell them that, but assure them that you and they can find out.

Chapter 10

Talking to Children About Foster Care

Removing a child from their family is always hard. It is never done unless people are certain it is the best thing to do, and no social worker makes the decision alone. However, even though you can know that the decision has been taken with care, it remains an often difficult and emotive experience. This is certainly the case for the child, but also for the parent(s) and the social worker.

How it happens will of course depend on the circumstances – a planned accommodation of a child can allow for preparation of the child, the parent(s) and the foster carers. An emergency accommodation on the other hand is more rushed, but it is essential still to keep the child at the centre, and the only way to achieve this is to be prepared. The best way to do this is to have an awareness of general things that you can do in advance of any child's accommodation. This should include youthinking about how to explain to children what is happening and also thinking about the practical things that are important to most children.

If a child has a social worker, this will be an indication that there needs to be change. Generally speaking, as the child is dependent on their main carer, we are going to be reliant on that adult to recognise the need for change, and then to make this change. The degree to which this will be successful will depend on the case, but as a social worker we cannot predict with any certainty the outcome of my work with a family. It is also true that life itself can be unpredictable and, as a result, we have learnt that it is best always to keep in mind the possibility of having to accommodate a child.

As part of any assessment, it is important to find out about wider family and friends, asking in detail if the child ever stays with these people, and whom they are close to. The use of genograms (family diagrams) are helpful and children usually enjoy making these. We will also do a genogram separately with the adults. Genograms are good practice in making assessments, but they also allow us to put feelers out to see if there would be a relative carer if ever required.

Getting to know the child

Another part of any assessment process is to find out in detail the child's routines and needs. With the possibility of accommodation at the back of my mind, I am going to find out the smallest detail. For example, if a parent informs me that the child has a special teddy I will make a point of being 'introduced' to that special bear, as I need to know what he looks like if I am searching for him in a hurry! I also want to know what role he plays – is teddy someone to cuddle up to, someone to tell troubles to? If he falls out of bed in the night, does the child feel able to retrieve him or do they need help because of the 'monsters under the bed'? And speaking of monsters and things that go bump in the night, do we need a night light on?

PRACTICE EXAMPLE

On beginning my assessment of Ann, aged 9, I noticed that she had lots of teddy bears on her bed. So many that it would be hard for her to fit into bed! I wondered whether this was just because she had acquired many teddy bears in her 9 years, or whether there was another reason. To find out, I brought my teddy on a visit and asked if he could meet her teddy bears. Leaving the door open, I sat on her bed and we played and chatted. Through this play I discovered that there were yet more soft toys under the covers who were in charge of a realistic-looking, but pretend, gun. Ann's army of teddies were protecting her from ghosts and a variety of scary creatures, which she knew about because she was regularly watching horror films with her mum. Obviously, we needed to address this with her mum, but I also knew that if Ann were ever accommodated then I would need to accommodate a lot of teddies too!

In asking about a child's fears, I also need to know what comforts them, and to see if I can establish from either the parent(s) or child where the fear stems from.

Knowing that a child goes to bed at 8:00 pm is helpful, but I also need to know what they do before bed. Do they go to sleep straight away, or do they enjoy a story to help them get to sleep? Do they sleep walk or get up in the night? Do they have bad dreams? What do they wear to bed? Do they wet the bed?

Thinking about personal care, does the child enjoy a bath or a shower and when does that happen? Who helps with hair washing and how often does that happen? Does the child get their teeth brushed? Do ask this question and others in this way – that is, don't make positive assumptions that these things happen. By checking out if they do happen, you allow a parent to say that they don't happen. You need to know the truth and not what the person thinks you want to hear, so be sensitive in how you ask such questions.

PRACTICE EXAMPLE

I previously worked within the travelling community, providing parent and child play sessions. A child was accommodated from the camp, and I contacted the social worker to see how they were managing and if I could help. The wee boy was aged 3 and generally coping well with being in foster care; however, he was always distressed when the carer tried to bath him. To me, who was familiar with the travelling community, the problem was obvious. Whilst there was a shower in the caravan where the child had been living, children were often washed in the sink. However, a bath was a new thing. Imagine facing that big expanse of soapy bubbles for the first time, especially at the age of 3 when your fears are starting to develop. Once the foster carer had this information, she began to offer showering instead. The social worker reported back a short time later that he was happy in the shower and managing fine.

In talking about food and meal times, again, be very open and sensitive to how you word questions. If a family eats takeaway every night, I want them to be able to tell me that. Similarly, if they eat toast and jam for two days before getting paid, I need them to be able to say that. You need to be able to convey that you are not judging. This does not mean that you are accepting or approving poor choices or that you won't try to guide or change, but that you will not criticise or judge. Food can be an emotive subject, particularly in the current age where there is a lot of education around healthy eating and people know what is right to do, but can struggle to put it into practice. This can be for lots of reasons, from breaking old habits to finances. In terms of future planning, if a child has grown up with ready meals, then home-cooked food might be quite a shock and will taste different. I find out favourites and dislikes/ allergies. If a child is then accommodated, at the very least we can make sure they have their favourite meal on their first night. If this is a takeaway or microwave meal, then so be it. Familiarity is more important than nutritional value on night one. A foster carer told me about a little girl whom she had been caring for. The carer had shouted that tea was ready, to which the girl argued that it couldn't be, as she hadn't heard the 'ping' yet. She had rarely had a meal at home that hadn't been microwaved. She initially didn't enjoy the taste of home-cooked meals and had to be weaned onto them.

Take lots of photos

It is good to have photos for a whole host of reasons. They are a great way of helping to build rapport and relationships. Giving a parent a lovely photo of their child is usually very much appreciated; providing a child with photos to make a collage about their family can be fun and stimulates talk; and photos are essential for memory books or life story work. They can also be used to make a pictorial timeline of a child's life. Often parents might take photos on their phones, and it can be helpful to offer to get these printed there and then as photos can get deleted or phones lost. Also, if a child does become accommodated, then these photos can become even more precious, and, at this point, parents may feel less able to work in partnership and therefore less able to give you the photos for their child's memory box or life story work.

Resources to have at hand to ease the process of accommodation include the following.

Paperwork

Ensure you have the relevant paperwork handy for the parent to sign before the child is accommodated. This will speed things up and allow the process to be quicker and calmer for the child. The process of being accommodated can be a long one depending on how it takes place and the location of foster carers. The child, and possibly adults too, will be physically and emotionally exhausted. Anything that helps is worth it!

Bags and bears

It is the policy of the social services department in Edinburgh, where the authors work, that no child's belongings should be put into black bags or similar, but rather should be packed into a proper travelling bag/suitcase. Using black bags or similar is degrading and conveys a lack of respect for the child and their belongings. Likewise, having a few spare teddies can be useful and, whilst they can never replace a much-loved soft toy, they can sometimes offer some small comfort and can act as a substitute for the child if their own toys cannot be accessed for whatever reason. You can also 'fill' the teddy up with cuddles – by hugging him in the child's presence and counting the hugs! The child can be told that they can then 'claim them back' from the teddy when they feel they need one. It's best you have some bags and teddies stored somewhere as there is rarely time to go and purchase them at the time of accommodation.

Carer's profile

The foster carers will have produced a child-friendly profile of themselves. If you are the social worker, remember to ask the foster carer's social worker for this profile. This should be a handmade book with photos that show pictures of all the family members, pets, the house and the foster child's room. There will often be snippets of information about the people in the house and the routines of family life. In this digital age, there really is no excuse not to be able to access these quickly and print them off so that you can go through this with the child. Knowing about where the child is going and seeing pictures will help the child (and parent(s)) feel calmer, and can also open up an opportunity to ask questions.

Books

Have some books or stories in your work bag that explain about being accommodated. If you are going to collect the child by car, leave one of these on the back seat alongside another book of general interest so that the child can find it and read it quietly if they wish. This could either be a story that you have written, or a published one. The advantage of writing your own is that you can personalise it to your area or even make it about you – so telling a story about you accommodating a teddy for example, and illustrating it with photos of that bear in your car, walking down a local street, etc. is a really nice way of making it real. If that particular bear can be in the car and with the book, most children will love that, and this makes a very gentle and child-centred way of opening up conversation around accommodation. It can be good for this book to remain available not just on the day of the child being accommodated, and the teddy (who perhaps also has his own suitcase with his belongings in the boot of your car) may even keep the child company for a time after they are first accommodated.

PRACTICE EXAMPLE

Jack, aged 8, had been in my car many times. Teddy and Elf were always on the back seat of the car and both had bags to look in and explore. Teddy had a cardboard suitcase with a towel, hair brush, pretend sandwich, his own teddy and a book about the day he went to stay with carers. Elf had different things in his bag and his pockets, mainly focused around emotional literacy.

Jack was a fairly streetwise boy, and would certainly not wish to be seen to be enjoying soft toys, but in the safety of the back seat of a car and out of view, he had lots of fun with them. He of course explored the bags and had read Teddy's story. We had talked about it and I explained that sometimes I kept children safe by finding people for them to live with if their parents were unable to look after them. Jack had been fascinated by this, and asked lots of questions before we moved on to talk about other things.

A number of months later, Jack's mum suddenly became seriously unwell. There were no family members who could care for him and he needed to be accommodated into foster care. When I went to collect Jack, I found a very frightened, tired and upset little boy.

Seeing his mum so unwell overnight had been traumatic for him and he was glad to see a familiar face and to receive a hug. At this point we had no identified foster carers for Jack, so there was no child-friendly carers' profile to introduce. However, I needed to tell him that this was the plan.

I acknowledged that his mum was sick and asked him what happened. He told me it all very quickly, in the rushed way that children can do when upset and needing to get it all out. Rather than focus on the detail of that at this point, I felt that it was important to reassure Jack by telling him about what would happen next. If their main carer is unavailable, children need to know who will meet their needs. Not knowing who the carers were going to be was an added complication and far from ideal, but the emergency nature of what had happened meant that it was perhaps not unexpected. I assured Jack that I was going to keep him safe and look after him. I advised that the first thing we needed to do was to sort out breakfast. Jack nodded. I then asked, 'What is your worry?' Note the assumption that there is a worry – this was deliberate on my part, and a good habit to adopt with adults and children is to ask this question routinely. Jack asked if he was going to be taken to school, saying that he didn't want to go in later because he would then get a row. We agreed that I would take him into school so as not to be late, and that then we would get breakfast in school (I had weekly sessions at school with Jack so this was a familiar routine to take him out of class). This child-centred practice meant that he could arrive on time rather than me reassuring him that it would be okay if late. Had I done the latter, Jack would likely have still been left with anxiety until he had got to school and experienced this as being okay. I listened to what was important to Jack and took into account his view of the world. Most importantly, I wanted to offer care to him that he would experience as me meeting his needs. In addition, when we were having breakfast I needed him to be able to focus on what I was telling him rather than him being anxious about being late.

After a quick face wash and comb of the hair, Jack arrived at school on time and he was able to line up and go in with his friends, something also important to Jack. Jack was in class at the start to hear about the plan for the school day from the teacher (important so that he knew what was happening in the day, as missing this can lead children to feel left out or at a disadvantage because they don't know what is happening). My school colleagues were happy to provide me with a small room and pull together some breakfast. I outlined to them the situation and was able to organise for Jack to be a helper in the nursery for the afternoon, something that he loved to do and which usually was given as a reward.

This meant that the afternoon would be less taxing for him as the day progressed and he became more tired. I collected Jack from class and we sat down to a feast of bananas on toast with milk. As we ate I explained that Mum would need to stay overnight with the doctors and nurses who would help her to get better, and I advised that I would take him to visit his mum as soon as the doctor said that this was okay. I explained that I would collect him from school and take him to stay with a foster carer who was a safe adult who knew all about looking after children and liked having fun with children. I explained that I would stay for a little while, but that I would then leave him and come back the next day to take him to school (it is important that children know when they will next see you as a key adult). As a social worker, I can't take a child to school every day but as part of the settling in process when they move to live with foster carers, I often do it on the first day, especially after an emergency accommodation. Jack replied, 'Oh like you did with Teddy – like his story.' I agreed that it was just like this. Jack replied, 'That's cool, so can I see the book about who they are then?' Well, of course I didn't have the book as at this point we didn't have identified carers. My tummy did a little flip – if I told Jack the whole truth it was only going to cause him worry, so instead I told him that I hadn't yet got it, but would hope to have it when I collected him from school. Jack's next focus, having read

Teddy's story, was that he did not have pyjamas with him or indeed a suitcase to unpack. From an adult's perspective, it would have been easier to advise that the carer would buy all he needed. However, Jack needed predictability as he was already coping with a lot. His only point of reference about accommodation was what he had read in Teddy's book. I therefore advised that I would bring a bag with me and that we would stop to buy what he needed. It would have been better for Jack to have his own things but we had no way to gain entry into the home at this point. Jack was satisfied and comforted by knowing what was going to happen next. The fact that Jack's experience was following Teddy's story gave him, to some degree, a sense of predictability, alongside the continuity of myself as a familiar and safe adult being with him. The routine and familiarity of school life also helped. Jack was keen to go back to the class to tell his teacher his news.

How to explain – language to use and language to avoid

First, know the child in question, as their developmental stage will dictate the language that you use. We know that many of the children coming into foster care will have language delay so, as a general rule, particularly if you don't know the child well, aim to use simple concrete language. Fewer words are better than more. In addition, try to mimic the child's use of language, so if they called their mother 'Mammy', then you call her 'Mammy' as well.

When talking about foster carers, don't refer to them as 'foster mum' or 'foster dad'. The child only has one mum and dad – their birth parents – and 'foster mum and dad' can be threatening to birth parents. Foster placements work best when birth parents work in partnership with carers. I also tend to avoid using the title 'foster carer' when speaking to younger children, as it doesn't mean a lot. Older children may also have preconceived ideas, planted by the adult world! A good rule to follow therefore is 'don't label, instead describe'. Therefore, in talking to a child about a foster carer I might say, 'Jen is a safe adult that I know. Just like me she knows all about how to look after children. She will make your tea, we can tell her what you like and she will help you wash your hair and take you to school.' To introduce the family you might say, 'Jen lives in a house with her little girl Amy and they have a cat called Topper. Jen and Amy have their own bedrooms, and there is a bedroom for you to sleep in too. Look, I will show you a book that they have made about them and their house.'

For older children, the content is similar but your approach will obviously be a bit different. For example, 'So I have found you a safe place to stay. You are going to stay with Jen and her little girl Amy – oh and they have a cat called Topper – he's great! Jen really enjoys spending time with young people and she will take good care of you. Why don't you have a look at this as it shows you pictures of their house and them – I think that window there is where your bedroom is; you will have your own space.'

In talking to children about why they are being accommodated into foster care, the truth is always best. It is also important to emphasise that it is not their fault that they have been removed from their parent(s)' care – this is a message that needs to be repeated over and over, by all the adults involved in that child's care. You may need to give this message throughout the child's placement, and afterwards. Children at the 'magical thinking' stage of development understand anything that has happened to them as being something that they have influenced, and will need particular reassurance. Sadly, a number of children have also been threatened with being 'taken away by social work', often when parents are trying to discipline them. This encourages the belief that they have been accommodated because they were 'bad'.

It is impossible to cover all the possible reasons for children being accommodated and explanations that therefore need to be given, as these are personal to the individual child, but below are some more general statements that you can use as a guide.

When a child has been physically neglected:

> An important part of being a [mum/dad] is to make sure that you have enough to eat, have clean clothes, that if you get sick you get taken to the doctor, that you go to school – and [Mum/Dad] hasn't done that. That is not your fault. So I need you to stay with [foster carer/relative] because I know that [foster carer/relative] can do these things for you (if neglect is caused by drug and/or alcohol misuse, then also explain that).

When there is danger of the child being hurt:

> [Mum/Dad]'s behaviour has been unsafe, and I have a big worry that you could get hurt. My job is to keep children safe and so I am going to take you to stay with [foster carer/relative] as I know you will be safe there.

When there has been sexual abuse:

> All adults know that it is not okay for them to touch children's [use language of child and to be specific about the child's experience, e.g. 'flower']. [Name of perpetrator] broke that rule and [Mum/Dad]'s job was to keep you safe but this didn't happen. That isn't your fault. I need to make sure that you are safe and that you live with adults who will keep you safe. I know that [foster carer/relative] understands the rule that your body belongs to you, and they will keep you safe.

At some point most children will ask questions about how long they will stay in foster care or with their relative carer. This can be difficult to answer because often we don't know. If you can give a concrete answer, then do tell them. But if not, try to give as much certainty as you can. For example, if a parent needs to show stability in their drug use, then realistically this is not going to happen in a couple of weeks. Therefore, you would try and give the child a sense of that, of what would need to happen before they went home, and who is responsible for this. This is a lot of information for a child to absorb, and it will need to be repeated and modified according to the age and stage of development.

A word of caution: the first time I had a conversation with an older child about this I tried to give them some certainty because they were constantly pushing for a time frame. I also wanted to help them to settle into their placement. I explained, 'You will be definitely here until after the summer holidays and then we will see how Mum is doing'. The summer holidays were 9 months away, and it was my aim to have the child home in 6 months. I was overoptimistic and naive. Mum did work hard and initially stopped using illicit drugs, but in the fifth month disengaged from the drug programme and relapsed in a huge way. The child was therefore not going to be able to go home after the holidays. As soon as I knew this I told them. However, they were so upset as they had held onto the words 'after the summer holidays', not hearing the 'then we will see' point, and had seen this as a concrete plan. I have never made the same mistake, as well intentioned and effective as it was in the short term (as it did help them to settle in placement), because it caused that child pain.

The following are activities to support talking about accommodation into care:

Activity: The Bridge or Stepping Stones
Purpose

- To facilitate conversations about transition, both in terms of the practical tasks and the feelings around transition. This activity is used when there is a planned accommodation or a planned move, for example, from emergency carers to long-term carers.

What you will need

- card – large sheet plus extra sheet for cutting out

- good-quality felt tip pens and coloured pencils

- scissors

- Blu-tack™ – or similar.

What to do

1. Preparation:

   a) Draw a linear picture (you want to invite the child to colour it/add detail with you of a river).

   b) On one side draw a picture of the place in which the child is currently living and on the other side draw a picture of the place where they are going to stay.

   c) Draw a bridge between the two places – the bridge is made of bricks and you should draw these in too.

   d) In the middle of each brick, write a task that needs to happen during the transition from one placement to the other. For example, 'Gemma needs to get your room ready', 'Have a goodbye party at Brownies and find out where my new Brownies meet.' The adult should do most of these before meeting the child, but leave some blank bricks for the child to give suggestions.

e) Cut out some small clouds (some with lightning), suns and rainbows. Onto each write a feeling. For example, the sun could be 'happy', the cloud 'sad', the cloud with lightning 'angry' and the rainbow 'mixed'. Place a little Blu-tack™ on the back of each.

f) Cut out small rectangles – one for each person involved in the transition process who will have direct involvement with the child. Keep it simple, for example, adult the child is living with, carer they are moving to, child. If you are the social worker, you may be the one consistent person – you will be there before, during and after the move.

2. Introduce the child to your picture and explain that you have drawn it just for them and that it is going to help you to talk about what is going to happen when they move. Invite the child to colour in the picture and to personalise it. Work on the picture together.

3. Notice the bricks or respond to the child's questions when they ask about them. Advise that we won't colour them in as that is a job for later and that you will explain in a while.

4. Invite the child to draw representations of the people in the rectangles. Stick little bits of Blu-tack™ on the back of each 'person'.

5. Invite the child to place the picture of themselves on the picture of the house that they currently live in alongside the pictures of the adults they live with there. Place the carers on the other home. Place yourself next to the child and say something such as, 'I am going to put me beside you because I am going to be there for you wherever you live.'

6. Acknowledge again that the child is going to move house. Looking at the bricks, talk about all the things that have to happen before it is time to move, and ask them if they can think of anything else. Any other things can be written on the blank bricks.

7. Ask the child if they can see anything that has already happened – you need to ensure that at least one of the bricks has, for example, 'Audrey has told me I need to go and live with [new carer].' When they have found it, invite the child to colour this brick in because this brick has been cemented in and has begun to make the bridge. Explain that when all the bricks are coloured in, the bridge will be fully built and it will be time to walk across and go and live in the new house.

8. Now look at the weather signs with feelings on them. Explain that the river is a river of feelings and stick all the feelings words in the river. Suggest that moving can bring lots of different feelings – sometimes one a time and sometimes lots together, and sometimes mixed up feelings. Referring to the brick that the child has coloured in, ask what feelings the child had when this happened. Ask them if they can pick a feeling and put it in the sky in the picture. Ask if there are any feelings that are not there, that need to be made.

9. The picture should stay with the child. Hang it up somewhere that is easy to access but not too obvious – perhaps on the back of a kitchen door. It acts as a reminder and the child can also be encouraged to fill in a brick between your visits if they and the current carer complete a task. The emotion in the sky may also change, and sometimes I make reference to the unpredictable weather of Scotland being like emotions that can change quickly. Each time you visit, work on or review this picture together. You may want to begin to move the picture of the child and yourself across the bridge as the bricks begin to be coloured. However, for some children it makes more sense to leave this until the end. The picture should also go with them to their new placement to allow the child to reflect on their journey, and can be used to show their new carer the journey they have been on.

Top tip: if the child is angry and upset, this picture may end up being on the receiving end of an outburst. This is of course an appropriate use of the picture, but children do usually regret destroying it. Take a photo, therefore, every week and if the worst happens you can print off a copy and carry on!

For younger children, you may wish to use stepping stones as a simplified version with less to complete. For example, (1) I see a picture of my new house and the people who live there and will look after me. (2) My new carers [names] come to visit me at my house. (3) My new carers [names] take me to the park for a while. (4) I go for tea at my new carers' [names] house. (5) I pack my bag. (6) I go to live in my new house. My new carers [names] will look after me now.

In addition, rather than drawing this as a picture, you can make a model. Use boxes for houses, real stones to step on and make little dolls or use figures so the child can enjoy stepping the figures onto the stepping stones.

Chapter 11

Talking to Children About Adoption and Permanence

Talking to children about adoption and permanence should always be done in the context of wider life story work about their life journey to date. At the point of discussing adoption and permanence, children should, therefore, already have an understanding in line with their stage of development of why they are looked after away from home.

The subject of life story work cannot be covered here, and there are a number of books that can offer an in depth look at this important aspect of working with children. However, a team of social workers (in which the authors both have worked) spent a session putting together a list of tips for conducting life story work.

Given that adoption and permanence are significant parts of some children's life stories, we have included these tips below:

1. Life story work is a process – you need to revisit it at different stages of a child's development, and at different points in their journey (e.g. at the point of moving to a permanent placement).

2. If you are working directly with a child for whom permanence might be an outcome, consider this from the first point of contact with a child and their family. Even if permanence or adoption doesn't happen, it is always good for children to have concrete memories from their life. Gathering photos and key information about birth family life is vital. The 'soft' information is crucial to balance out the predominantly negative information held by social workers. This might include why their name was chosen for them, at

what age they met certain milestones or funny stories about things they said or did as toddlers.

3. Good preparation is key – have a plan of what you are going to do and how. However, be prepared for things not going to plan!

4. Start with the present when undertaking direct work, as this is the safest place for a child, before thinking with them about their past.

5. Think carefully about the time and location of working with a child, as this work can be emotionally tiring.

6. Keep copies of work you do (and date it), so that children are always able to access a new copy. It isn't unusual for a child to deliberately damage parts that they find difficult.

7. Find a way of including adoptive parents/long-term carers, and help them to feel able to continue undertaking life story work once you are no longer working with them.

Communicating with children about this subject can be complex. The processes involved in adoption and permanence can be confusing enough for an adult to understand, the subject matter is likely to be emotive, and it will nearly always involve significant loss and change for that child.

For children moving into permanent care, there are a number of stages that need to be considered. These can be grouped loosely into the following:

1. Revisiting why the child is looked after and accommodated, and considering with them why the decision has been made that they can no longer go home.

2. For children able to understand, they should be helped to understand the legal system behind permanence, particularly if the birth family are opposing this decision and/or the child has to give consent to this process.

3. If relevant, the issue of the child needing to meet and then move to permanent foster carers/a kinship carer or to adoptive parents. This will include loss of current carers, and

possibly loss of direct and/or indirect contact with the birth family. It may also mean separation from siblings or change in/loss of contact.

Being looked after and accommodated/ not returning home

Imagine that you woke up one morning and didn't remember how you had got to where you were in life: how you had met your partner, how you had come to live where you do and what was happening for the key people in your life. This can be what it is like for children who don't know and don't understand their life story to date. They may not understand why they have ended up living with carers who aren't their parents. Whilst you or someone else may have told a child in the past, this does not necessarily mean that they will either understand or remember what they have been told. This is particularly the case for children who may have been told different and conflicting information by birth family members, or for children who have only been given this information on a few 'one-off' occasions. As children tend to place themselves at the centre of what happens to them, they may also see their accommodation into care as their fault, and will need ongoing reassurance that this isn't the case.

In order for children to have a coherent narrative of their life, information needs to be honest, appropriate to their stage of development and given in a way that allows them to offer their memories and views.

- Avoid statements that are unclear and can be misleading. Adults can sometimes try to avoid difficult or taboo subjects. Children have a right to know information that has had a significant impact upon their life, and this will always be the case when children are unable to live with their birth parents. Unhelpful phrases include describing a person as 'ill' when talking about their drug use, or saying that a person has 'passed' or 'gone to sleep' when talking about their death.

PRACTICE EXAMPLE

Seven-year-old John had moved to live with his paternal aunt as a result of his father's drug use. Family members had sought to protect John from the truth of his father's drug use because they thought he was too young to be told. Instead, John was told that his dad was 'poorly' and therefore couldn't look after him. Several months later, John's aunt then became ill and was in bed for a week. John's behaviour at school deteriorated and he was refusing to come to school in the morning. It was some time before people understood the reason for this change in behaviour: John had associated being 'poorly' with moving to new carers and thought that his aunt's illness would lead him to have to move. The adults around John realised that John needed to be given accurate information about his dad's drug use, and that this could be done in a sensitive and developmentally appropriate way.

By this time, John's aunt had recovered, and with support, she was able to talk to John about what adults had meant when they said that his dad was 'poorly'. She explained to John that many years ago his dad had started smoking a drug called heroin. She explained that this drug made his dad feel very good immediately after he smoked it, but that his dad was then very sleepy. John's aunt explained that when his dad had smoked the heroin he wasn't able to safely look after John. She went on to explain that, though John's dad tried to stop using heroin, he was addicted to this. She explained to John that addiction was when someone felt that they had to keep doing something, or that they couldn't cope without it. To the surprise of John's aunt, he had a good understanding of his dad's drug use, and was able to tell her about times that he had seen his dad under the influence of drugs. By providing a full explanation, John was able to speak about his experiences and not feel that the subject was taboo.

- Ensure that the information you give a child is provided with reference to the child's lived experiences. This will allow it to be meaningful to them and to help them to make sense of those experiences. The following is an example of how information was given to a child whose mother experienced mental health problems. These difficulties impacted upon the mother being able to meet the child's basic needs. The child had told her social worker that she remembered her mother spending many days lying in bed, crying:

> Doctors said that Mum had depression, a word that means that Mum often felt sad and cried. When Mum was sad, she spent a lot of time in bed and found it hard to do things. Mum wasn't able to give you what you needed such as getting you to school, and making sure you had food to eat.

- It may be helpful to use the model of words and pictures, as developed by Turnell and Essex (2006). An example of how this would work can be found below. The advantage of using such a model is that children can add their own views and thoughts by drawing speech bubbles, and where there is difference in views this can also be presented. Also, the story can be developed over time as the child's journey continues.

Megan is 8 years old and lives with granny Jo and Lola the dog.

Until Megan was 6 years old she lived with her mummy Susan

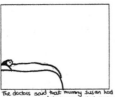

The doctors said that mummy Susan had depression, a word that means that mummy often felt sad and cried. when mummy was sad she spent a lot of time in bed and found it hard to do things.

Because she had depression, Susan wasn't able to give Megan what she needed, such as taking Megan to school and making sure Megan ate regular meals.

Megan's teacher Mrs Braid and her social worker David were worried about Megan missing a lot of school and being hungry.

Megan, mummy Susan and social worker David went to a meeting. mummy Susan agreed that granny Jo would look after Megan.

- Children need and have the right to know who the key decision-makers have been, and how their voice has been heard in this. They should be made aware of how decisions have been made and by whom. The section below on legal processes can help with this. If the child's view is different to that of the decision made, there will need to be exploration of why this is the case.

- Children may have been told that they will be listened to, and that their views are important and will be taken into account. An explanation of what it means to listen and to take their views 'into account' is important, as children may think that it means that what they want to happen will indeed happen.

- Allow children to have space to ask questions. This might include clarifying some information about the past, or about the future. When being told that returning home is no longer an option, questions might include asking whether they will still see key people in their life and what else might change. You might want to use a Worries Box for the child (see the activity at the end of this chapter). Often these conversations naturally occur when you are making a life story book with the child.

Legal systems

Using diagrams and flow charts can help children understand the decision-making forums and legal processes that have been involved. The use of words and pictures could also be helpful here. Visiting key places such as court or a Children's Hearing (in Scotland) might also be helpful, or using photos to remind children of places where they have been. Be mindful that the court may provoke difficult memories or associations for some children whose parents may have been imprisoned. In addition, children may have a simplified and skewed understanding of what happens in court, particularly through exposure to television and films. They may think that going to court will always involve going to prison and thus be worried if they think that their family will be discussed in court.

PRACTICE EXAMPLE

The following diagram was used to help an 8-year-old child understand the decision-making forums behind them becoming permanently cared for in foster care. This needs to be done alongside other work that explores why such decisions were made. This is based on the Scottish system and thus is different to other countries' legal systems, but can be adapted to where you work and the situation for the child.

The diagram is deliberately kept simple in order that you and the child can draw/write extra information in each box or at each arrow. This might include the reasons why the child became looked after and accommodated, and why rehabilitation didn't work.

Speech or thought bubbles can also be added in order to allow the child to put their thoughts and feelings in for each stage.

Moving to permanent carers/adoptive placement

Jo and Janette had been in foster care for almost 2 years. At the ages of 4 and 6 they had an age-appropriate understanding of the reasons why they couldn't be at home. In the past week, the court had agreed with the council's application for the children to be adopted. Whilst the foster carers had been very committed to the children, they did not feel able to adopt them. As the social worker to these children, I had a number of difficult things I would need to explain to them:

1. that the foster carers they had lived with for a significant part of their lives would no longer be caring for them. This involving answering 6-year-old Jo's question, 'Why can they not look after us until we are big and big?'

2. that I would be needing to find a new family for them who would look after them

3. that they would no longer be seeing their birth family and needed to move school and nursery.

It is worth pausing for a moment to note that this process can be emotionally tiring for all involved. This is obvious in the case of the children who are having to deal with uncertainty and limited control over their lives. Techniques for supporting this are discussed below. The fact that this is a difficult process for children impacts workers and carers too. Foster carers may also be coping with their own feelings of loss around saying goodbye to the children. For social workers, there is also the process of 'finding a family' for a child and this can bring a sense of significant responsibility as you give your views on proposed families. It is important to recognise this, as talking to children about moving to permanent care can be another emotionally difficult process.

Jo and Janette could not stay with their foster carers despite this being what they wanted to do. However, by involving children fully in the process, they are able to feel more in control of their future and are more likely to buy into this process.

1. 'Why can they not look after us until we are big and big?'

This has to be one of the hardest questions to answer, and needs to be met with honesty as well as allowing children the chance to articulate or express their emotions surrounding this. For children who have experienced rejection in their past, this may be a particularly sensitive subject. This may include explaining that some foster carers only look after children until they can either return home or go to live with permanent carers or a new family. Obviously, some children may have experienced foster carers choosing to commit to some children long term but not others, and in these cases, it can be helpful to talk about finding the best match for everyone involved. The activities 'Cuddly Toy' and 'Interview' can help to illustrate this. Jo found this whole subject particularly difficult and was angry with her foster carers. The carers were supported by their social worker to manage this and understood that this period of time was particularly difficult for Jo. Jo was also reassured that her foster carers would come and visit her at her new home after she moved.

2. Finding a new family

The family finding process is a really good opportunity for children to be and feel involved, and also to have a part in decision-making. It can also provide them with something to 'do' in what can feel like a long waiting time between being told that they will be moving and the process actually happening.

There are a number of activities that I have used with children of different ages, including 'Cuddly Toy' and 'Interview' (Chapter 11). The 'Worries Box' activity (Chapter 11) is also useful at this stage. In each case I have started with the premise that, on the one hand, the child is needing (a) new caregiver(s)/parent(s) to be in a family, and that, on the other hand, there are adults who want to be in a family but don't have children to care for. I explain that part of my job is to find the best caregiver/parent for that child, and that I need the child's help in doing this.

3. Endings with birth family/school/nursery, etc.

Moving to new carers will often involve multiple losses of key people in the child's life. Children accommodated in local authority care or in kinship care may have already had to experience multiple losses and changes at the stage of being accommodated. For children who have experienced inconsistency or chaotic lifestyles prior to being accommodated, this may be particularly difficult. This is also the case for some children with additional support needs, such as autism spectrum disorders or attachment disorders. Care needs to be taken to minimise the impact of such changes:

- Identify with the child who the key people in their life are. They may not always be the most obvious people to you as a professional or carer, and thus you need the help of the child to ensure that you are not missing anyone out.

- Explore with the child what activities or events are important to them to continue or not miss. I worked with a child who was moving at the point of finishing primary school. The child needed to move schools but we arranged for her to still go to her primary seven residential trip and to her leaving party, which was important to her.

- Speak to key agencies such as the school teacher or activity leaders. How can the child's leaving be marked? You may arrange in advance for peers to write goodbyes in a message book, or arrange a 'photo booth' so that the photos taken can be put into a memory book.

- How can any ending be done in a way that the child can manage? Some children will not have had positive experiences of endings and may struggle to manage an event that puts focus on them. Engage the child in deciding what they want to do but be mindful that, as the time gets nearer, children may not be able to manage this and may sabotage such events. A backup plan may be necessary for such times, and give the child the opportunity not to attend an ending.

- Keep endings short as a child is likely to struggle the longer this goes on. With the birth family, emotions will be heightened for all involved and thus a short activity may take the focus off this being the last contact. Think in advance about how all family members will be supported, and how the end of the last contact will be organised. How will the child leave and who with? How will the family leave? Do you need additional people present to support this? What risks are involved in this ending? Does this need to take place in a secure environment or can it take place in a public place?

- Be mindful that a child may need support after an ending. What this looks like will depend on the child. For some this may be the opportunity to run off energy, or it may be that they require a quiet environment with limited stimulation. They may need someone to talk to or may find engaging with others too difficult.

Activity: Worries Box

The Worries Box can be used effectively alongside the story *The Huge Bag of Worries* by Virginia Ironside (2011). Alternatively, the child may choose a bag like the one in the story or choose to make a drawstring bag – the disadvantage of this is that it is less easy to decorate.

Purpose

- To help children feel able to ask questions or write down worries they have.
- To help children manage difficult feelings.
- To help adults around a child to understand the key concerns for a child and therefore put in supports around them.

What you will need

- *The Huge Bag of Worries* book or to be able to tell a similar story
- a box (this can be any size, shape or material and can be chosen by the child if they wish)
- art materials (optional)
- paper or card
- pen(s).

What to do

1. Spend time with the child getting to know the story of *The Huge Bag of Worries* and talking about how we all have worries, especially at times of change and uncertainty.

2. Explain to the child that the information you have been giving them (i.e. about adoption/permanence) might have been difficult to hear and that they might have some worries or some questions. Explain that you have a special box in which they can put any worries or questions they have. Then, each time you visit there will be an opportunity for them to bring out anything they have put in there, and to talk together about them. The child can also be reassured that it is okay to share their worries with any of their safe adults.

3. I have used a box from a craft shop that is about 10 cm square, and have spent time decorating this box with the child. We have then cut up pieces of card or paper on which the child can write or draw their worries or questions.

4. The child then thinks up a very good safe or private place for their box where they can keep it until they want to share it. If the child is quite young, it can be helpful to have a practice at putting down a question or idea so that they get the idea of how this can work. It is important that you stress the importance of this being private and the property of the child to the caregivers in the house. I did this exercise with a child in foster care and due to the other children in placement, it was agreed that the box would sit high up in a cupboard in the kitchen so that other children wouldn't see it and read what was written inside. When I came back the following week, the carer told me that she had looked in the box to read what was written down. Whilst well intentioned, this undermined the child's right to privacy and to feel safe to write down her worries, and she never used the Worries Box again.

5. Before leaving, remind the child of when you are next visiting and that you will ask them if they want to bring out their Worries Box. It should always be the child's choice as to

whether they wish to bring it out and also which adult they wish to share their worries with.

Worries Box variation
Purpose

- To convey that everyone has worries.

- To allow the child the opportunity to name their worries.

- To allow the child and adult to make an immediate plan on how to 'fix' the worries and have a way of reviewing progress.

What you will need

- *The Huge Bag of Worries* book by Virginia Ironside (please note the National Society for the Prevention of Cruelty to Children (NSPCC) can provide free small copies so children can keep one)

- good-quality felt tip pens

- A4 paper.

What to do

1. Read and enjoy the story together.

2. Draw out some worry characters (if you make them like Mr Men you are along the right lines). If the children themselves can draw them, then this is better. There are also some templates at the back of the book that you can use.

3. Give the worry characters names, that is, what the worry is.

PRACTICE EXAMPLE

I received a police report outlining a call from a neighbour the night before. The neighbour had reported that the parent was taking drugs and was 'high'. The parents had a 9-year-old called Josh in their care. When the police attended, Mum appeared able to care for Josh but the home looked cluttered and there was concern about hygiene. The school had called the morning after the police visit to report Josh himself as having very poor personal hygiene and to be presenting as angry and upset. Josh was a new pupil and he was not engaging with the school staff. The school had none of his records and Mum was vague about her last address and Josh's last school. I was on duty and went out to interview Josh as there was an immediate concern for his welfare.

I brought with me to the school a large puppet, playdough, pens, paper, *The Huge Bag of Worries* book, some beads and other art materials, and some bubbles. I also brought some healthy snacks and juice.

Josh arrived with the head teacher. He was screaming swear words and kicking out. The head teacher guided him into the room and then closed the door. Josh immediately went under the table and sank his teeth into my ankle! Flinching a bit but determined to be positive, I thought, 'Well, I am not being ignored, I've got engagement!' Out loud, I said, 'Oh I think a little dog must have come to play with me because if it was Josh he would know that children don't bite.' Leaning over I noted that, whilst I still had a mouth on my ankle, I was not being bitten. I gently patted his head (barely touching but making a patting action) and said, 'Hello little doggy, aw, you're nice.' I slid off my chair onto the floor – half under the table – and said, 'I wonder, do you like stories?' 'No' was the firm reply. Taking my big puppet out of my bag, I said, 'Aw well, Elf does.' Most children love Elf, and Josh was no exception. At this, I began to read *The Huge Bag of Worries*.

As I read, I began my assessment of Josh's physical care. He had by this point leaned into me, and I noted head lice crawling through his hair. They were of various sizes and nits were also present. This told me that they had been there a while. Josh had blond hair and I could see his scalp was red and scratched – another indication that this was not just a stray louse!

I noted an unwashed body smell, no socks, shoes that looked tight and clothes that were unclean. Josh was also thin. I paused in my reading and went into my handbag, taking my packed lunch out. I offered it to him (guessing that some raisins might not be enough). Josh hesitated, but I smiled and nodded. He ate two cheese salad sandwiches, a banana and a pack of crisps in minutes. I continued to read. By giving Josh food I was meeting one of his basic physical needs. Not only would food help him feel better, it was giving Josh a strong message that I cared about him and understood what he needed.

At the end of the story I explained that everyone had worries, even me. I explained that I was a safe and helping adult to which he stated, 'Aye, you're a social worker, the head said' (I tend to describe my job rather than give a title). I stated brightly, 'Right, let's draw some worry characters and see if you can name them for me.' Josh shook his head. 'Na, Audrey.' 'Aw well, I am going to draw one for me', I said, and proceeded to do this. Josh advised, 'if you draw them I will name them'. I gave him a big smile and said 'right, deal!'

'Give me a high five!' He did this. I did this so as to increase our physical proximity albeit briefly – creating experiences that are shared is the beginning of developing a relationship.

Josh named his worries: 'nae clothes', 'nae food', 'Mum sleeping all the time again', 'nae pants and socks', 'heroin (the dealer with the gold car and the red cap is back)' and 'no DS' (his mum had put Josh's game console in the pawn shop and Josh didn't think he would get it back). Once he had exhausted his list, I reviewed them with Josh. I firmly believe that when children are brave enough to share a worry then they want action, so I was assessing what I could do immediately to help Josh. This would demonstrate to him that I was listening to him. 'Right', I said. 'I am going to the shop now to get you pants and socks, and when I come back you can put them on in the toilet. I will come and visit you and Mum after school and I will bring some food with me.' I explained that only Mum can sort out the heroin and the sleeping all the time, as well as the worry about the dealer, but said that I would offer to help her. It is important to be honest about what you can and can't do.

We agreed that I would keep Josh's worries safe with me. I did a home visit at the end of the day. I brought with me a bag of groceries, which included some cat food as Josh had told me about his little cat. He told me that he had told the cat his worries. Pets are often very important to children and can be great allies in keeping you as a safe adult to support the child.

Sadly, there was no option other than to accommodate Josh into foster care that night. A couple of days later I went to visit Josh and I took his worry characters with me. I was fairly confident that I would be able to get rid of the food, pants, socks and clothes worries and I was working on the DS problem. 'So Josh', I said, 'these worry guys are very noisy'. He smiled. 'I wonder if there are any we don't need anymore.' 'No', he replied with force and certainty. 'Oh', I said. 'I thought…well now, let's see, now is there food here (indicating the foster carers' home)?' Josh replied, 'It's great. I get breakfast, lunch and tea and I can have snacks too.' 'Good', I replied, 'so maybe we don't need the "nae food" worry anymore?' Josh maintained that we did. 'Oh, can I ask why?' I said. Josh replied, 'Because the plan will be to rehabilitate me back home again so I think you better laminate it.'

Once we got Josh's records it was clear that he was right. He had been accommodated and rehabilitated a number of times, with Mum moving around Scotland. This time, he wasn't rehabilitated home but was placed with a relative carer long term. Josh has allowed me to keep his worries, not because he needs them anymore, but so I can show other social workers and teach people about this activity.

Activity: Interview
Purpose

- To help a child be and feel involved in the process of family finding.

- To help professionals to understand what is important for a family to know about the child.

- To start introductions between a child and new family.

What you will need

- paper and pens, or digital audio recorder, and paper and pens.

What to do

1. Explain to the child that in order to help you find a family for them, you need their help. Depending on the individual child, this may be best done using paper or pens or a digital audio recorder (most organisations will have an audio recorder that can be borrowed for this purpose). For one child who enjoyed football, we discussed first how football players give interviews on the radio and that I would be 'playing' the interviewer and he the famous footballer.

2. Explain that it is important that you know all about the child in order to find the right family. You might also explain that there are things that the child might want a family to know about them as well. Come up with a list of questions that you are going to ask the child. Ask the child if they have any questions they think you should ask them. Some examples are listed below:

   a) What is your favourite/least favourite food?

   b) What football team do you support?

   c) What is your favourite subject/least favourite subject at school?

   d) Who is in your family?

   e) What is your favourite animal?

   f) How would you describe yourself in three words?

3. This can also include what the child thinks is important for their new family to be like. When this was done with a child who was moving into permanent foster care, she told me that they needed to be a family who gave her meals. This reflected her anxiety that she wouldn't be looked after properly, and work was then done to reassure her regarding this.

4. Either in the same session or another session, set the interview up. If this is done on paper, it can be set up to include space for writing, drawing or circling objects. For example, Jo and Janette were too young to write down answers for what their favourite activity was. Therefore, a number of pictures of activities were printed, and Jo and Janette drew a circle around the activities that they enjoyed doing. If using the digital audio recorder, you might want to spend time playing with this so that the child gets used to it, and you may wish to act it out as though you were on the television or radio interviewing someone famous. Add to the fun by using a fake microphone or dressing up.

5. With the child's permission, you can give this to the permanent carers, and this can provide a good starting place for conversation between the carers and the child.

Activity: Cuddly Toy (this works best with children who are at a younger developmental stage)

Purpose

•   To help a child be and feel involved in the process of family finding.

•   To support a child to think about their feelings in respect of the process of family finding.

What you will need

•   a cuddly toy animal (preferably an animal favoured by the child)

•   pens and paper.

What to do

1. Start by explaining to the child that just as they are needing a new family, you have a special someone who also needs a new family. At this point bring out the cuddly animal, and explain that they have no one at the moment to look after them as they are not able to live with their mum and dad.

2. At this point the child might want to ask why, and this can be an opportunity to invite the child to provide their own answers with respect to this. You may also give reasons to mirror the child's situation. I also ask the child to tell me what name they would like to give the animal, and maybe spend some time playing with the animal with them.

3. Ask the child whether they would do something very important for you and foster the animal until you can find the animal a new family. This can include discussing where the animal might sleep, and thinking about what the animal might need whilst they are in 'foster care'. At this point you 'speak' to the animal to explain that they will be living with the child until you can find them a new family.

4. Depending on the needs of the child, this might be all that is done on this visit. The next stage, whether at this point or at a future visit, would be to ask the child about what they think the animal's new family should be like. This might include some topics such as 'games that they like to play', or 'whether they like pets or not'. This can be written down or drawn on paper if you wish. You need to be careful that you are not setting up unrealistic expectations; therefore, you might want to help shape responses. For example, a child who said that they would like the animal's family to have a swimming pool, might be told that swimming pools are very expensive, but how would it be to say that the animal's family need to like taking the animal swimming?

5. Future visits can use the animal to elicit feelings and thoughts around the prospect of moving to a new family, and at the stage of moving. The animal becomes a third object that allows a child to express their own feelings and thoughts in a safe way.

6. When the child has moved to their new family, you can ask the child whether they think that their animal could also live permanently with their new caregivers/parents. The animal can continue to be used in order to elicit the child's feelings around the move to their permanent family.

Chapter 12

Talking to Children About Mental Health Problems

Mental illness remains a stigma in society and something that people struggle to speak about. As children grow up they are likely to have come across adults with mental health problems and may have found these adults' behaviour unusual or frightening. They may have experienced such adults being laughed at as well. Recently, I was taking the bus home from work. One of the passengers on the bus was singing out loud to herself, making up the words and tune as she went. She had mental health problems and I understand that she did this to self-soothe. However, some of the other passengers could be seen whispering about her and pointing to her. The two women next to me started laughing at her. There is little tolerance in society for those who are different. The language used in society is also unfavourable to people with mental health problems, with words such as 'mad', 'crazy' or 'nuts'. Older children may also have been exposed to media stories that portray those with mental health problems as dangerous. It is likely, therefore, that children will have been exposed to some level of negativity in relation to mental health problems, and this should be borne in mind when talking to a child about this subject.

Before talking to a child about a person who has a mental health problem, familiarise yourself with the condition in question. The Royal College of Psychiatrists has an excellent website with leaflets for both young people and adults. These describe a number of mental health problems as well as there being leaflets that also explain different treatments available. They also reference other websites particular to each condition.

As with any other subject, ensure that you work in partnership with the main caregiver(s) and/or the parent(s) to agree on what information should be given to the child. It is also helpful to gain an understanding of how the condition is experienced by the person in question. Whilst each mental health condition will involve a variety of symptoms, which symptoms manifest and how these are experienced will be individual to the person. If the child is living with a person with a mental health condition, or has spent a lot of time around them, they will also be able to present their lived experience.

How to explain

When talking to children about a mental health problem, it is important to consider what is happening on a physiological level and also what is seen behaviourally. Even very young children will understand that sometimes our bodies don't work as they should and that when they don't work properly, we can become unwell. This is a helpful approach to explaining mental health problems as well. The following activity can be used to explore mental health problems.

Activity: Poorly Brain

Purpose

- To help children understand what it means to have a particular mental health problem.

What you will need

- pens

- paper

- colouring pencils or good-quality felt tip pens.

What to do

1. Start by asking the child if they can think of a time when their body wasn't working properly or they were ill. This might be because they had broken a leg, or because they had a cold. If they don't come up with one, I would suggest

using something like a broken leg as this is an easy example to illustrate the point.

2. Using the child's example, ask the child to draw a picture of what they looked like when their body wasn't working properly.

3. First, explore with the child what was happening inside their body. For a broken leg, that would be that there was a break in the bone, or that the bones weren't all straight. For a cold, this would be that there was virus in their body and their body was fighting to get rid of it. Write the words inside the body on the picture (or for younger children draw a representation).

4. Next, explore with the child what you could see on the outside that would show their body wasn't working as it should. For a broken leg, that might be a cast or it might be that they couldn't put any weight on the leg. For a cold, it might be that they had a runny nose and kept sneezing. Write these words round the outside of the body.

5. On a new piece of paper, ask the child to draw a picture of a person. Explain to the child that having a mental health problem is just like the example they gave, as it is about when our bodies don't work as they should.

6. Explain that just like other parts of the body, the brain can sometimes not work properly. Introduce the name of the person you are talking about, and explain that they have an illness that is called [insert name of illness].

7. You then need to explain what is happening in the brain. The type of illness will dictate how you explain this. A mood disorder (e.g. depression or bipolar affective disorder) could be described as the brain producing too much of one emotion; for example, feeling sad or feeling super energised. A psychosis could be described as the brain telling the person things that are not true; for example, hearing things that no one else can see, or seeing things that aren't there. Encourage the child to ask questions about this, and/or to tell you what

their experience of this is. Write these words; for example, too much sadness, inside the head of the person.

8. Next, explain that just as you might see someone with a broken leg not being able to walk because of the crack in the bone [use the child's example], so we see things on the outside when someone's brain isn't working properly. Encourage the child to name what things they have noticed. Examples might be that someone with depression has a brain that is producing too much sadness, and therefore they are lying in bed a lot and crying often.

9. Someone experiencing mania might not be sleeping, might be talking very fast, and not making sense to other people. If the child does not know, support them to understand what behaviours they can expect to see from this person when unwell.

10. Finally, take time to look at the picture and ask them if there is anything not written down that they want to ask about, or if they have any worries about what is written down. Use curiosity to sensitively explore this; for example, 'I'm wondering how it might feel to be around someone who is [name of behaviour].'

Explaining to children what can help someone with mental health problems

It is helpful to again draw attention to similarities between physical health problems and mental health problems. This helps the child to understand, but it also reduces the stigma associated with mental ill health.

I would explain that just as someone with a broken leg would have to see a doctor, so someone with mental health problems might have to see a doctor. If the person in question has been admitted to psychiatric hospital, then again this can be described in comparison to a general medical hospital. If an adult is taking medication, this can be explained as a way of making their brain work better. If an adult is going for counselling, this might be explained as them talking about difficult things that are getting in the way of their brain working as well as it should.

At times, people can be admitted to psychiatric hospital because they present a risk to themselves or other people and, as a result, there may be particular rules about this hospital that means that the child cannot visit/the person cannot leave the ward/the ward might be locked, etc. If this is the case, the child may need reassurance that they will be kept safe if visiting, and may need support to express any worries they have. An explanation might be that:

> The brain tells us how to behave and how to keep ourselves safe. For example, when we think about crossing a road with traffic on it, our brain tells us to wait until there is no traffic around and it is safe to cross. Because [name of person] is unwell with [name of illness], their brain isn't working as well as it should and so isn't always telling them how to behave and how to keep themselves safe. That is why they are having to stay in hospital/we can't visit/the ward is locked – the adults around them are having to keep them safe until their brain starts working properly again.

PRACTICE EXAMPLE

James and Sarah were 8-year-old twins who lived at home with their dad. The parents had recently separated, and the children's mum lived nearby; the children split their time between their parents. The police were called out after a neighbour was concerned to see the children's mum, Barbara, behaving in a strange way late one night outside the house. When the police attended, Barbara was standing outside the house brandishing a knife. She was experiencing visual hallucinations. The children's mum was admitted to psychiatric hospital, where she was diagnosed with schizophrenia. The children were very upset by the incident that night, having seen their mum's strange behaviour from inside the house. This was further exacerbated when they came to visit their mum in hospital and she appeared to be speaking to people who were not there. She begged the children and their dad to help her 'escape' and became distressed when they left without her.

I was introduced to James and Sarah by their dad John as someone who could help them with any questions they had about their mum. John felt that the children would be more open with someone outside the family than with him, because of the parents' recent separation. We started out playing some drawing games before James made reference to the recent incident outside their house. I asked James and Sarah if they felt able to draw what happened and they both drew a picture of the house with their mum outside. This helped me to gain an understanding of how each child had experienced that incident, from thinking that the police were there to arrest their mum to worrying about why Mum was behaving in a strange way.

James and Sarah were helped to understand that their mum's brain wasn't working properly because of an illness called 'schizophrenia', and that she was in hospital so that the doctors could help her brain work better again. James and Sarah had only a little bit of experience of their mum being unwell, but we explored what they had seen. For example, they learnt how this illness in her brain meant that she could see things that weren't there and hear noises that other people couldn't. By talking about some of the other symptoms that people with schizophrenia can have, they were able to give examples of how their mum had acted in a paranoid way, putting cameras up round the house.

Using the 'Worries Box' activity (Chapter 11), James and Sarah were able to express their worries and ask questions as time went on. Mum was discharged from hospital but, unfortunately, did not take the medication and on a number of occasions their mum attended at the house in a very unwell state. James and Sarah continued to use their Worries Boxes, but also needed support to cope with how they felt about what was happening. The 'Emotions' activity in Chapter 14 and the 'Words and Pictures' tool explained in Chapter 11 were also very useful to use with James and Sarah. Mum continued to be non-compliant with medication, and contact between the children and their mum was therefore supported by a safe adult always being present.

How we describe some of the more common mental illnesses to older children and young people

Depression

Depression is an illness that makes people feel sad and tired almost all the time. Sometimes people who are depressed feel worried and can't think of how to get help with their worries or how their worries can get fixed. Sometimes, someone who is ill with depression finds it hard to sleep or they might sleep a lot more than normal. Someone who is depressed finds it difficult to do things every day. Everybody can feel sad and a bit down sometimes, but someone who is ill with depression feels like this a lot of the time and it goes on for a long time. The doctor can give medicine to help with depression and talking to a trained counsellor can help too.

Phobia

A person has a phobia if they are very scared of something like snakes or spiders, or sometimes people are afraid of other things such as leaving the house. Someone with a phobia might be so scared and afraid that the fear stops them doing things that they like. For example, a person with a phobia of snakes might not be able to go to the zoo. Somebody called a psychologist can help people with phobias. Psychologists understand the way people think, behave and feel.

Psychosis or schizophrenia

Psychosis is an illness that can make people behave in a strange way. The person might see, hear, touch or taste things that are not there. They might believe things that are not true. For example, they might think that they are being watched or followed, but have no real reason for this to be true. Another example is that someone might think they are someone else such as the Queen or a famous popstar. A doctor called a psychiatrist can help people with psychosis or a diagnosis of schizophrenia. Sometimes this is by giving the person medicine or sometimes by helping people to learn ways to cope with this illness.

Neurosis

People who experience neurosis can find that everyday things cause them worry. They might, for example, panic when the doorbell rings or they might get very angry very quickly, and for no reason.

Obsessive-compulsive disorder

People who are obsessive-compulsive can feel very worried about something and believe that if they don't act in a certain way then something bad will happen. For example, a person might think that if they don't use bleach on the toilet every time they use it, then germs will grow and make them ill. Another example is that a person might have to check that they have locked the door a certain number of times. A psychologist can help people who have an obsessive-compulsive disorder.

Anorexia

Anorexia is an illness where the person worries a great deal that they are too heavy even when this is not the case. The person who has anorexia will worry so much about being too heavy that they will try very hard not to eat, and they might make themselves sick after they have eaten. They also might exercise a lot in order to make themselves as light as possible. People who are anorexic are often very thin and can lose so much weight that their body stops working properly. Despite this, when an anorexic person looks in the mirror they are not happy with what they see and still believe that they are too heavy. A psychologist can help people who are anorexic.

Chapter 13

Talking to Children
About Dementia

It is estimated that there are 850,000 people living with dementia in the UK (Prince *et al.*, cited by Alzheimer's Research UK). This equates to 38 per cent of the population knowing a family member or close friend living with dementia (YouGov survey, commissioned by Alzheimer's Research UK). It is further estimated that 1 million people in the UK will have dementia by 2025 and that this will have increased to 2 million by 2050 (YouGov survey, commissioned by Alzheimer's Research UK).

Dementia is devastating for any family to face. Adults often feel distressed observing changes in the affected person's behaviour, and a loss of ability and independence. Family members will likely experience feelings of grief and as though they are gradually 'losing' a loved one. For a child it can be a very confusing and difficult thing to understand, both in terms of seeing changes in the person with dementia and also seeing the stress and distress of other family members.

As always, the best place to start is to be open to talking about the subject in a child-friendly way that is appropriate to the child's age and stage of development. However, to do this you will need to have at least a basic understanding of the illness, which should also help you to appreciate the child's lived experience. Below is a basic outline – we do emphasise that the authors are not experts in dementia. There is a wealth of information available that is far more comprehensive than we can offer here, but the below should be enough to enable you to talk to children about the subject.

General overview

- Dementia is an overall term that describes the symptoms that occur as a result of a disease of the brain.

- There are many types of diseases that cause dementia but Alzheimer's disease and vascular dementia are the most common ones.

- Not everyone will experience the same symptoms and, at the start of the illness, changes are less noticeable.

- These diseases are progressive, meaning that symptoms become more pronounced over time, gradually impacting more and more on everyday life.

- The rate of progression is individual to each person.

- These diseases are considered to be terminal illnesses, as at this time there is no known cure. However, many people die of complications caused by the disease or another unrelated illness before they die from dementia.

Symptoms of dementia

- Memory loss – not being able to recall things that have happened very recently, and eventually not recognising loved ones (people can often, however, remember things from long ago).

- Difficulties in carrying out everyday tasks that require sequencing, such as cooking a meal or getting dressed.

- Cognitive difficulties including loss of the ability to solve problems and rationalise.

- Difficulties in concentration such as difficulty in watching a television programme from start to finish or completing a task.

- Difficulties in making decisions, for example, asking what someone wants to eat may be too difficult for them, but giving them two choices might be manageable. At a later stage this may in itself be too difficult.

- Difficulties with language. This can include struggling to find the right word or needing time to process language. The individual may struggle to follow a conversation, may repeat the same thing often or have standard questions that they ask repetitively. At a later stage, the individual may withdraw and not communicate with language.

- Fluctuation in mood or a change in normal demeanour. For example, someone who has for most of their life presented as laid back may change to become more dynamic and more easily stressed. Heightened anxiety is also a common experience for people with dementia.

- Behaviour changes such as walking a lot, packing and unpacking, being less in tune with social norms and less socially appropriate, repeating actions or routines.

- Experience of delusions – seeing or hearing things that are not there.

- Visuospatial skills becoming impaired, for example, finding it hard to judge the height of a step, seeing the pattern on a carpet as holes or reaching for an item and knocking it over.

- Orientation – losing track of the time of day or date, and confusion about where someone is.

- Loss of muscle tone and mobility.

What might be the child's lived experience? What might they find especially hard?

Obviously there are a lot of variables in answering these questions! The child's age and stage of development, their general nature, the affected person's stage of illness, the relationship the child has had/has with the affected person and how the wider family are coping are just some of these variables. Given the variation, we can only really write from a general perspective and hope this will point you in the right direction!

Loss

Children, like adults, will often experience a sense of loss. The affected person may have been someone who used to look after the child, someone who was seen as a strong and powerful person who could protect the child, or someone who could make things happen. For a child to find that the person can no longer do these things is initially confusing. Then, as they understand that this person has gone forever, grief follows.

Frustration

It is not uncommon for children and adults to feel frustrated by the person with dementia. One child, aged 10, complained that 'She doesn't even remember my name' when talking to me (Audrey) about his granny. Names are very important to children, and he was very hurt that his name had been forgotten. The same child also experienced his granny agreeing to play a game with him. He went to get the game and, on coming back, Granny stated that she did not want to play, and furthermore maintained that she had never agreed to play in the first place. Children don't manage well with inconsistency. Naturally, he felt frustrated and that this was unfair.

Embarrassment

One young person aged 14 stated that she was 'not going out with her again. It was so not cool.' She went on to tell me that her gran had spoken to 'everyone' and that 'Even when they tried to go away she just kept talking and wouldn't take the hint.' Sometimes caring for someone who is becoming less socially aware can be challenging for both the adults and for the child. As a teenager, there is often a felt need to conform with peers. Children and young people also have a template of how they expect adults to behave. Therefore, an adult who is behaving in a socially inappropriate way can be very challenging for them.

PRACTICE EXAMPLE

I visited a café with a 6-year-old child and their granny, who has dementia. Everyone chose what they wanted to eat, but by the time the food arrived, Granny had decided that she no longer wanted the scone she had ordered. In retrospect, I think she tried to tell me this but verbal communication was a difficulty she experienced. In sheer frustration, Granny ended up throwing the scone over her shoulder in favour of the slice of cake chosen by the 6-year-old. Fortunately, Granny was sat with her back to the wall so no one was hit by the flying scone. However, the sheer look of horror on the 6-year-old's face mixed with indignation that her cake had been 'stolen' was some sight. Whilst I wanted to laugh, I gently reassured her that we would get her another slice of cake, and affirmed that, no, it was not okay to throw scones at walls.

Once settled again, the child asked, 'So what is Granny's consequence going to be?' So now I had a dilemma. For this particular 6-year-old, behaviour and consequences are big subjects that need to be brought up on a regular basis. Should I try and explain that Granny's illness means that we need to give her a bit more leeway, or should I keep it simple? Given the age and stage of the child I decided to keep it simple, asking her what she thought the consequence should be? The 6-year-old gave this some thought before announcing her decision: 'Well, she don't remember so good now, so maybe she forgot the rule about not throwing stuff. So I think we would just forget it.' Ah, the wisdom of children. How big was my smile as I replied, 'I think you're right.'

Boredom

Children can get bored when they are asked the same questions all the time, but often want to be respectful to the loved one. This can leave them finding it hard to extract themselves from this situation, and sometimes just not being able to have a flowing conversation is difficult.

Overwhelmed

Being with someone whose mood fluctuates or whose temperament radically changes can feel overwhelming and sometimes frightening for a child. To see a previously calm and safe adult being angry, and on occasions for nobody to truly understand the reason for the anger, can be scary. Children will also often blame themselves: 'She is always angry with me, I must be doing something wrong.'

Talking about dementia

The breadth of problems/presenting difficulties that dementia brings, and the fact that you cannot 'see it', means that it can be hard to explain. I think that it is important to work with what is happening now – so find out what the specific symptoms are of the person whom the child knows.

Activity: Let's Get to Know Dementia
Purpose

- To create an opportunity to talk about dementia.

What you will need

- pens
- large sheet of paper
- soft drawing pencils
- eraser.

What to do

1. Ask the child to draw a big picture of the affected person. As you do this, talk about that person. Talk about what they like, what the child likes about them, what they enjoy doing together and whether there is anything that the child doesn't like. Also explore whether the child has noticed any changes in the person.

2. A discussion about age should then follow, speaking of how the body changes as people get older. Even if the person with dementia is young chronologically, they will be older than the child (you may remember being a child and thinking that someone in their 40s was old, and someone in their 60s

ancient! Our concept of what is 'old' tends to increase as we age). Explore first the changes we might see as someone gets older, such as hair colour changing, getting wrinkles or using a walking stick. Then start to talk about things that are less visible but often talked about, such as having aches and pains, or not being able to see as well.

3. Finally, draw a very simple picture of the brain. Explain that the brain is responsible for all our learning and remembering – use your knowledge of the impact of dementia on the person the child knows and also draw on what the child has said about the changes in the person. Explain that these things are all to do with the brain not working so well now.

4. Choose one particular issue that the child has highlighted – for example, a person forgetting a name. Write that name inside the picture of the brain and then, using a soft eraser, rub it out. The eraser represents the dementia taking the memory away and parts breaking off, therefore causing disease.

PRACTICE EXAMPLE

You will remember the story of the boy who was upset that his granny did not remember his name. I invited him to write his name so that it was quite bold (using a soft lead pencil) inside the picture of the brain. I then took a soft rubber (the kind that crumbles easily) and explained to him that the rubber was called dementia, and that it is a horrible illness that does this. At this point I began to rub the name out, at first just lightly so you could still see it, though not clearly. I then rubbed it out completely. I moved all the crumbly bits of rubber into all the other areas of the brain, and explained that all the crumbly bits were getting into the brain and clogging it up, stopping other parts working too. I explained that this affected his gran's behaviour, ability to make choices, etc. The boy replied, 'So it's like all the bits of dementia breaking off and clogging Gran's brain up so it doesn't work well.' I agreed and acknowledged that it was not fair. We spent a few minutes talking about how much we hated dementia.

The example above is obviously not a scientific or medically accurate explanation. However, the important things it explains in a fairly visible way are:

- The changes the child sees are caused by dementia, which is an illness in the brain that they can't see.

- It is not the affected person's fault – it is dementia's fault, and it is okay to be angry with dementia.

- It is a progressive illness.

Storytelling

Sometimes stories can also be helpful to tell children. *Grandad Mac Moves In* is a story that I wrote for a younger child to enable us to have a conversation about dementia. You are welcome to photocopy it and maybe invite the child to draw pictures to match the story. You could also write your own story.

Grandad Mac Moves In: A Story about Dementia

Iain went to visit his Grandad Mac every week. Sometimes he went with his mum and dad but often, because Grandad lived close by, he would go on his own.

Grandad Mac was great fun! He had an amazing collection of very old toy cars that he allowed Iain to rearrange in the cabinet.

In the summer, Grandad Mac would take Iain out to the garden and they would plant seeds together. Grandad Mac knew everything about plants – all their names, what they needed to grow well, how to prune them – just everything! He enjoyed teaching Iain and, whilst sometimes Iain thought to himself, 'Boring!', mostly he really liked learning. And it was always good when he could impress his teacher.

The other part of going to visit Grandad Mac was that Iain enjoyed helping his grandad out. He would go to the shop for him, help him put the things away, and maybe do the hoovering for him. As he would leave, Grandad Mac would always go into his top pocket and pull out a £2 coin. 'There you go son', he would say, 'that's for you!' There would be a big smile and a hug before Iain left Grandad Mac, who would be waving at the door. Iain would then go to the shop for sweets, and make sure he ate them before he got home so that he didn't need to share them with his sister Janet.

One day Iain went to visit Grandad Mac as usual, but Grandad wasn't in a very good mood. 'My glasses have gone, son. I can't find them anywhere!' Iain helped Grandad look for his glasses, and they eventually turned up in the fridge! Iain thought that was very odd indeed but it didn't really matter because Grandad was happy again.

They watched TV together for a while, before Grandad invited Iain to rearrange the cars in the cabinet. Grandad Mac's favourite car was the red mini but Iain preferred the blue three-wheeled car. Iain did a bit of hoovering for Grandad and, as usual, Grandad Mac gave him his £2. 'Thanks Grandad. I am going to buy some highland toffee.' 'Well mind and watch your teeth, son,' said Grandad, 'or you'll end up with wallies like me!' They both laughed as Grandad pulled out his false teeth.

The next day as Iain came in from school he heard Mum and Dad talking at the kitchen table. 'I am worried about him; he keeps losing things,' said Mum. 'Aye, and he is always in a fankle. He's just not himself,' said Dad. At first Iain wondered who they were talking about, but quickly he realised it was Grandad Mac. 'I found Grandad's glasses in the fridge!' joined in Iain. 'Oh dear,' said Mum. 'I think something's up.'

The rest of Iain's week was fairly normal. After school he went out to play, trying to catch fish at the burn before going on the rope swing. It was good playing outside but he also liked when it rained, as it was a good excuse to play Minecraft for hours on end. He decided to show what he had built in one of the Minecraft worlds to Grandad Mac.

After tea, Iain asked Mum if he could go and visit Grandad Mac. Mum agreed and asked Iain to make Grandad some toast for his supper. Iain knocked hard on Grandad Mac's door before opening it and shouting, 'Hiya, it's only me.' But there was no cheery answer from Grandad as there normally would be. When Iain went into the living room, he could almost not believe his eyes: all of Grandad's old toy cars were scattered across the table, and Grandad was looking very, very angry. Iain had never seen his grandad look so angry, and he felt a wee bit worried. 'SOMEONE HAS STOLEN THE MINI!' shouted Grandad Mac, shaking his walking stick in the air. At first Iain thought that he had better go and get his mum, thinking that she would need to get the police if someone had stolen from Grandad. But just then Iain noticed the red mini in the middle of the table. Taking a deep breath (and feeling a bit brave because Grandad was so angry), he went and picked it up. 'Grandad, is this the one you've lost?' A big smile came over Grandad's face as he replied, 'Aye aye son, it is.' Together they put all the cars back into the cabinet. Iain tried to show Grandad Mac how Minecraft worked but he didn't really get it so Iain decided to go and make his grandad toast. However, Iain couldn't find the bread for ages. He eventually found it in the oven, and found the butter in the bread cupboard. Everything seemed to be very mixed up!

Iain did the hoovering and was really surprised and disappointed when Grandad didn't pull a £2 coin out of his pocket. 'I wonder what I did wrong,' thought Iain. 'Maybe I didn't do the hoovering very well.' But Grandad Mac still gave him a big hug and a wave when he left. 'Oh well,' thought Iain, 'I can't be that bad then.' But Iain still felt sad and upset. Grandad Mac just wasn't the grandad that Iain knew.

When he got home, Mum and Dad were busy. Janet was in BIG trouble as she had left the gate in the bottom field open, and so all the sheep had got out. Dad was already tired from a day's work on the farm and he was not happy at having to round the sheep up. He was giving Janet a row, and mum had her 'this is serious' face on. 'Best not interrupt,' thought Iain. So he went to his room to play Minecraft, but his niggly sad and worried feelings would not go away.

And they stayed with him the next day too. By the time he had been to school and come home again, he was really down in the dumps. And it was about to get worse.

Mum was at the table and he could tell she had been crying. Dad looked all serious. 'What's wrong?' asked Iain, feeling alarmed. 'Now it's going to be okay, but Grandad Mac had a little accident this morning, and he is in hospital,' said Dad. 'What's wrong? What happened?' asked Iain. 'You've not to worry, your grandad's okay, but he left the cooker on at lunch time, and the potatoes boiled dry. There was a small fire and he burnt his hand,' Dad explained.

After tea, Iain, Janet, Mum and Dad went to visit Grandad Mac. His hand was sore and he seemed a bit muddled, but he smiled when he saw Iain and Janet. They sat up on his bed and watched TV with him.

Grandad stayed in hospital for quite a long time. Mum explained that the doctors were doing lots of tests to see if they could find out why Grandad Mac had been a bit different lately. Iain visited every week with Mum and Dad. He got to know the different nurses on the ward, and Grandad always had a smile when he saw Iain. One day as they were leaving, Grandad took a shiny £2 coin out of his pocket and gave it to Iain. 'But I've not done your hoovering for you,' said Iain. 'That's just for you being you,' replied Grandad with a smile.

On Saturday morning, Mum asked Iain and Janet to come and sit at the kitchen table. She had baked a big chocolate cake. 'Dad and I have got something very important to tell you,' said Mum. 'Grandad Mac is going to come and live with us.' Iain was really happy. Janet asked whose bedroom he would have. 'Nobody's,' replied Dad. 'We are going to make the dining room into Grandad's bedroom and get a new downstairs bathroom where the washing machine and dryer is.' Janet clapped her hands and Iain smiled even more. 'When's he moving in?'

'Well,' said Mum, 'as soon as we get the bedroom and bathroom sorted, but that won't take long. But I have some more news. Do you remember Grandad was getting lots of tests done? Well, the doctors have found out what's wrong. Your grandad is ill – he has dementia.' 'What's that?' said Iain.

Mum explained that it meant that Grandad Mac's brain was not working properly. She said that it meant that he forgot things easily, that he will get muddled up, and that some of the things he used to do easily might now be difficult to do. 'He needs me to look after him now, and I might need your help sometimes. Do you think that you could help me sometimes?' 'Yes,' said Iain and Janet together.

'So when Grandad put his glasses in the fridge and thought someone had stolen his red mini when it was still there – that was because he was ill? It was the dementia's fault?' asked Iain.

'Yes, that's right,' said Mum. 'Grandad will lose lots of things, and he might get really cross sometimes or get muddled up about things, and that's the dementia's fault – it's because Grandad is ill.'

'It's going to be really good having Grandad living with us. It will be a lot of fun a lot of the time,' said Dad, 'but some days it's going to be hard. If you feel upset or you've got a question, you talk to Mum and I, right?' Janet and Iain both agreed they would.

'Right Iain,' said Dad. 'You and I have a special job to do. We need to go and get all of Grandad's special cars and his cabinet, so that we can set them up in his room. Then he will feel at home.' 'I think we should bring his chair too,' said Iain, 'and his bookcase because he loves his books. Especially about the plants.' 'Good idea,' said Dad.

In a few weeks' time when the bathroom was fitted, it was time for Grandad to move in. Janet loved the new bathroom, which was called a 'wet room'. It meant that you could splash about in the shower as much as you liked because the floor and walls were all waterproof – like at a swimming pool. For Grandad it meant he didn't need to climb into a bath – his bones were old and he was a bit stiff! A lady came to visit – her job was as an 'OT', which stood for occupational therapist. She worked out whether Grandad would need handles to hold onto in the bathroom and also gave Mum a high toilet seat to fit on the toilet. Iain and Dad joked about this being Grandad Mac's throne and Iain even made him a crown so he could be king of the bathroom.

Another man, who was a social worker, came to visit too. He spoke to Mum for a long time. Mum explained that he had arranged for a carer to visit to help Grandad to have a shower, and also for Grandad to have a holiday at a care home every month. The social worker said that this was called respite care, and Mum said that at these times, they would go camping. 'Grandad wouldn't manage in a tent now,' said Mum.

Dad went to hospital to collect Grandad Mac and Mum, Iain and Janet put up balloons and made a cake to welcome him home. Iain made sure that the red mini was at the front of the cabinet where Grandad Mac could see it. They had put Grandad's chair by the window so that he could see the birds and the sheep outside. Janet made sure the cushions were in place and comfy. Everybody was excited that Grandad was coming home.

When Grandad arrived home with Dad, he smiled and was pleased to see his red mini and his own chair. He was tired and had a sleep whilst Mum made his favourite tea of steak pie. Iain woke Grandad when it was teatime. Grandad was a bit muddled. 'Where am I? Who are you?' he asked Iain. Dad was right there. 'It's okay

Grandad Mac, remember you are home now. Iain your grandson has just wakened you because it's teatime.' 'Right,' said Grandad. Iain thought it was a bit strange that his grandad hadn't known who he was. 'It's okay,' said Dad. 'Remember that is the dementia's fault.' 'Okay, but I don't think I like dementia,' replied Iain. 'I don't like dementia either,' replied Dad.

Tea was a bit different from normal. Mum had to help Grandad Mac to cut up his food, and Dad needed to remind him to have a drink. Iain had to rescue Grandad Mac's fork out of the milk jug as Grandad seemed to think that this was a good place to put it. But everyone enjoyed the steak pie, there was a lot of chatting as normal and, most importantly, Grandad Mac seemed much happier. After tea, a man called Dave arrived. He helped Grandad Mac have his shower and get his PJs on. 'Wow,' said Janet, 'Grandad Mac gets ready for bed earlier than me!' At bedtime, Mum helped Grandad into bed and Janet and Iain went to kiss him goodnight. 'It's cool having Grandad at home,' thought Iain. 'Even if he does some different things, like putting the fork in the milk jug!'

Supporting the relationship/finding shared activities

Whilst we can empathise with the difficulties that children experience, it is also important to help them understand that they still can find things to enjoy with the affected person, so that neither they nor the individual in question miss out. As a general rule, younger children tend to be more accepting, with older children perhaps struggling with this a little more.

It is important to remember that, in the early stages of the illness, dementia will probably not interfere with the relationship between the child and the affected person. It is important that this relationship is maintained. As the illness progresses, however, the person's ability will lessen and their behaviour will change. It is likely that at this point, the child will need support to get to know this 'new' person. It can be fun finding new activities that both can enjoy.

Music
Music can be a great source of pleasure whether listening to it together, playing percussion instruments or children dancing to the

music. This can bring a lot of enjoyment to all – try to provide a variety of music. The child can be responsible for changing the music and trying to find the adult's favourite song. Do sing too!

Photos

Looking through old photos together, sticking photos into an album and writing down any memories about the photos can be a positive experience for both child and adult. It can also be helpful to take lots of new photos, and make scrapbooks about current experiences too. You can now buy lap trays that have a picture frame top – placing photos of family members with their names written on them can be very helpful and children will enjoy making these.

Collage

Children may enjoy making a collage of a favourite thing. So, if the adult with dementia loves dogs, then they may decide to cut out lots of pictures of dogs and stick them onto sugar paper to make a collage.

Skills/hobbies

If the person with dementia had a particular skill or hobby that may not have completely diminished, then this can be focused on. For example, a lady I know with dementia was a great baker. She can no longer bake independently but she loves to mix the ingredients. So, when her grandchildren visit they follow the recipe and weigh the ingredients, but Granny does all the mixing! Tasks such as doing the dishes, washing the car or folding the washing can be done together, and young children usually like the idea of being responsible for helping an adult to do a job.

Tasting sessions

I have found from experience that dementia can affect the person's taste and the textures that they enjoy. As a treat the child may choose to bring a variety of foods, cutting them into little pieces and having a taster session to see if they can discover any new favourites. It can also sometimes trigger memories. On one occasion, the person with dementia tasted some toffee and spoke of how she had melted toffee over the fire to make a bigger but thinner piece to share. She explained how she had done this as a child during the war, when sweets were rationed. The child was fascinated to hear about this as he had been learning about World War II at school, and was then able to tell the class this story.

Personal care

Sometimes people with dementia will enjoy doing activities that they used to do, such as brushing a child's hair. The child may also enjoy combing the person's hair and soon, a game of 'hairdressers' has started. Likewise, older children might enjoy giving a hand massage and applying nail varnish to the person in question.

Whilst these are a few suggestions of activities that children can do with the person affected by dementia, it should not be underestimated how much can be gained from just spending time together, and the person with dementia may simply enjoy watching the child playing around them.

Chapter 14

Talking to Children About When Someone in the Family is Unwell

This chapter is written out of the knowledge that many children will need to come to terms with a loved one becoming unwell. This may be an older member of the family such as a grandparent, the child's parent(s), a sibling or the child themselves. The uncertainty that comes with serious illness, the complexities at times of medical processes and procedures, and the fear of death can leave adults uncertain of how to approach discussions with children.

There are a number of fantastic charities in existence that can support families when someone is very unwell, and some of the children's hospitals also offer play therapy to support a child who is unwell (and at times siblings). The authors recommend that families take advantage of these where possible, and that professionals seek their expert advice where appropriate.

It is of course always important, where possible, to speak to the child's main caregiver(s)/parent(s) to come to an agreement about what needs to be said. It is also helpful to establish what the child has already been told. Though it may have been well intentioned, children may have been given information that is unclear or inaccurate, and this might need to be readdressed when talking to them. It may also be advantageous to speak to medical professionals and understand better the situation for the person who is unwell. This may include establishing what the medical condition is and what this means for the person in question, what treatment will be involved (if any) and the prognosis. Obviously, whether this can be done or not will depend on who the unwell individual is (and whether they have given consent to this), and your role/relationship with the child.

When a family member or loved one is seriously unwell, there will be significant stress in the family. Approaching the child's caregiver(s)/parent(s) needs to be done sensitively. When faced with such stress, a coping mechanism may be to minimise or deny how unwell the individual is. Therefore, the adults may find it incredibly difficult to agree to a child being told how unwell someone is. In such circumstances, acknowledge the adult's position whilst exploring the need for a child to have a developmentally appropriate understanding.

Whatever you agree should be said to the child, it is crucial that you don't give a message that you don't know to be the case. For example, do not tell the child that the unwell person will get better if you don't know that is definitely the case.

Let the child know that they haven't caused this illness. Children may blame themselves for the person being unwell, whether this is a family member or even themselves. This is particularly the case for developmentally younger children.

Children tend to dip in and out of conversations. It is important that the adult goes with this and remains child-centred. Depending on the developmental stage of the child, they may not be able to take on all the information at one time, and will often need to hear the information on more than one occasion. Allow the child to have space to go off and play, and don't be surprised if there is no immediate reaction from a child on you giving them difficult information. Alert school and other key people to the fact that the child has had difficult news in case strong emotions play out in different settings.

Be prepared for difficult questions. It can be helpful to consider what questions a child might ask before you sit down with them, so you can be prepared to answer them. At the same time, if you don't know, it is okay to say this to the child. You (and the child) can agree to find out this information for them. Offer an opportunity/space for the child to come back to you with questions. By bringing up the subject again at a later time, it shows the child that it is okay to talk about this. The activity 'Worries Box' in Chapter 11 would be helpful for this. You can also use a puppet or soft toy that has lots of pockets/places to put little pieces of paper. The child could put any worries or questions in these places, so that it is the 'puppet' who then finds them and asks the question or says the worry as though it is theirs. This can feel easier for a child than them having to 'own' their worries or questions.

Prepare the child for seeing the ill person, particularly if they might have a lot of hospital equipment around them; for example, tubes and monitors, or if the person is going to look different, for example, without a limb, no hair, etc. This might include the child being able to play with a soft toy that is made to look like the ill person, for example,with tubes, bandages, etc. You might also be able to show a photo of the person in hospital, or allow the child to phone the person before visiting (this demonstrates to the child that this is still the same person). If the person who is ill has a caregiving role, then you will need to explain to the child any changes that this might involve, for example, a mum being unable to physically pick up the child any more, and what the person (or someone else) might be able to do instead.

One of the taboo subjects in society is talking about death. It is important that when death is going to occur, or is a likely outcome, this is acknowledged with the child so that they are able to process this. With young people, you should advise them that death is a possibility if that is the case. If this is not discussed, and then a loved one dies, the child has no opportunity to mentally or practically prepare themselves for this. The child may have a number of questions around this, such as whether death is painful (particularly if they are the person who is unwell), and what happens after death. If the parents wish to give a concrete answer as to what happens after death, based on their beliefs, then supportive adults should reinforce this message. However, it is also acceptable to answer this question by giving choice, for example, 'Some people believe this...others think...I am unsure, etc.'

The use of small world sets such as Playmobil® or Lego® can be helpful for children to explore the information they have been given. Both Playmobil® and Lego® have hospital sets. The authors have on occasion made up church/funeral sets with papier-mâché — be creative! The benefit of these is that children can feel a sense of control over what happens in their play. They can explore different outcomes in a safe and non-directive way.

When the child is ill

When talking to the child who themselves is ill, the child will normally know themselves that something isn't right. This might be because they feel unwell or because they have had a number of hospital attendances or admissions. The following is a list of things you need to consider when talking to a child:

- Don't underestimate children's awareness of what is happening. Often adults can think that because the child doesn't say anything, the child doesn't know. When children are in hospital, they will overhear conversations between adults about them. The unfamiliarity of medical terms is likely to be confusing for the child as well as overwhelming. In addition, children will speak to the other children on their ward and this may also provide them with information that they are ill-equipped to deal with, if they haven't been spoken to about their own situation. I (Becky) previously worked with a group of children who all had cancer. For many of the children, they were responding to treatment and it was anticipated that they would fully recover. A couple of the children knew that it was very unlikely they would recover, either because they had not responded to treatment or because they were on a waiting list for a transplant that never came. Imagine a child has been newly diagnosed with cancer and admitted to a ward with these children, but has not been given a full and age-appropriate explanation of their illness and what it means for them. That child's understanding of their future will be very different depending on whether they speak to a child who is likely to recover or a child who is aware that they are terminally ill.

- When speaking to a child about their illness, use the correct medical terminology; for example, cancer, sickle cell anaemia. Then explain what this is in age-appropriate language. For example, for a very young child you might describe breast cancer as a 'bad lump' that needs to be taken away to stop it getting bigger and making the person very poorly. For a young person, you might explain that everything in our body is made up of 'cells'. Cancer happens when the cells in our body don't work as they should, growing too fast and stopping the normal cells in our body from working properly.

- Remember that you don't need to wait until you have all the information about the illness in question. It is very likely that you won't know everything and that there will be uncertainty about the trajectory of the illness – it is okay to say that you don't know everything yet, and that you will keep the child updated as they go.Be honest with children. If something is likely to hurt or make them feel worse, it is important that the child is aware of this. For example, if you tell a child that an injection won't hurt and then it does, they are unlikely to trust you when it comes to something more significant. It is much better to say that it will hurt and then work on distracting them and rewarding them for being brave afterwards. Children value your attention and care.

- Be honest with children. If something is likely to hurt or make them feel worse, it is important that the child is aware of this. For example, if you tell a child that an injection won't hurt and then it does, they are unlikely to trust you when it comes to something more significant. It is much better to say that it will hurt and then work on distracting them and rewarding them for being brave afterwards. Children value your attention and care.

- When speaking to a child about what has happened or is going to happen next, you may wish to use pre-existing books on the subject. Online websites for bookshops categorise books under topics such as 'personal and social issues' or 'social stories'. Charities in relation to particular illnesses will also be able to point you to specific books that they recommend. You may also create your own story for the child, either doing this for them or with them. For a child who enjoys drawing, make a book out of blank paper and put either one or two sentences on each page. As you work through the book, the child creates a drawing for each page of text, and as they do this you can explore this part of the story with them. Questions might include, 'How do you think [name of character] is feeling just now?', 'What questions do you think [name of character] might have for the doctor?' and 'What would help [name of character] just now?'

- Another technique for supporting a child to understand what has happened/what is to happen would be to use a soft toy or puppet as the unwell child, and then act out what is to happen/what has happened. Medical interventions such as the use of a stethoscope, injections or having a cannula put in will be at best experienced by children as stressful, and at worst frightening. Where possible have toy equipment that represents the real equipment that is going to be used, such as a plastic stethoscope, thermometer, plasters or bandages. These can be used to play out the procedure on a soft toy and then on them afterwards. These can also be used for free play, which allows the child to play out their experiences and/or fears in a safe way. If a child is going to be admitted to hospital in a planned way, you might want to visit the hospital beforehand so that the venue is familiar to them. A number of hospitals have leaflets for children that help to explain what will happen when they come into hospital.

- Create a sense of normality, limits and boundaries. Limits and boundaries can sometimes be abandoned because the adults are feeling sorry for a child or feeling guilt in the case of siblings. However, children need the normality and boundaries in place. If boundaries are removed, then this can create anxiety; children need to feel contained.

- Allow 'normal play' including messy or active play, if at all possible given the child's illness or situation. Encourage school links to be maintained. This might include seeing friends, still getting homework, use of software to chat online, posting pictures so the child can keep up to date with what is happening at school, etc.

- When talking to children about what will happen, empower them as much as possible. This includes allowing them to take control where they can over personal care, being able to make choices over medical procedures where possible (e.g. site of injection, choice of plasters, etc.). When personal care has to be done for a child (from 3 years on), ensure that they have choice over who is allowed to help with this, get adults to seek permission each time, ensure that adults who do not need to be in the room leave when personal care is given.

- Explore with the child what familiar items they could bring in, if in hospital. Where possible, think about how they can personalise their space, make choices about food and think about what food adults may be able to bring in for them.

- Bear in mind that the child may try to take on a caring role for adults in their family. They may not want to upset them, and feel that they have to be brave. Give them the message that it's okay not to be brave and to be afraid. Acknowledge that the child may have a number of different emotions, including anger, and give permission for the child to feel these. The following activity can support this.

Activity: Emotions

Purpose

- To help children to explore how they feel about a difficult life event.

- To build emotional literacy.

What you will need

- blank paper

- good-quality felt tip pens.

What to do

1. Start off by explaining that when people hear difficult information they can have lots of different emotions. Ask them to name what emotions people might feel when they hear that someone they love is unwell. You could make this even more specific to the information the child has been given; for example, that Mum is going to have to have an operation so that the doctors can remove the cancer.

2. Write these all down on a piece of paper. Be mindful that a child may feel that there are certain emotions that are not allowed such as 'jealousy' or 'anger'. If these are not named but you think they are relevant you might want to say, 'I know

that sometimes people can feel [name of emotion]. Is it okay if we add this one as well?'

3. Explain that these emotions are a bit like cartoon characters; for example, Mr Happy, Mr Angry – and that they look different, have different personalities, they do different things, etc.

4. Ask the child to choose one of the emotions they have written down and explain that you are going to get to know this emotion really well. Take a page with a pre-drawn person on it, and either you or the child write the name of the emotion at the top.

5. Explain that just as the cartoon characters all look different, emotions also look different. Ask the child what they think this emotion looks like. You might ask them what animal the emotion might be if it were an animal, or what colour the emotion would be. Using blank paper the child might wish to draw what they think the emotion looks like.

6. Next, explain that just as emotions look different, they also feel different from each other. Ask the child what they think the emotion feels like in different parts of the body. If the child is struggling, guide them through this with statements such as, 'How does your face feel when you are angry?' or 'How does it feel in your stomach when you are sad?' Either write the words or draw the words inside the person on that particular part of the body.

7. Once this is complete, ask the child what a person might think or say when they feel that emotion. Then write the words inside the head or coming out of the mouth of your drawing. An example might be, 'I hate you cancer' for the emotion 'angry'.

8. Finally, explain that all emotions act differently. Ask the child what people might do when they feel that emotion. Write or draw these things outside of the outline of the person. An example would be that when they are sad, people might cry, put music on or go and talk to someone. This is also an

opportunity to explore with the child what might be helpful to do when they feel this emotion.

9. Repeat the above steps with as many emotions as the child wishes to do. Bear in mind that this might be a difficult activity for the child and, therefore, consider how the child might be able to wind down after the activity. This might include chatting about something fun, undertaking a nurturing activity such as reading a book or having a snack, or running off some energy at the park.

PRACTICE EXAMPLE

Seven-year-old Anna had been struggling at school with her reading and was holding electronic devices close to her face when using them. The school suggested to her mum and dad that Anna would likely need glasses and that they should take her for an eye test. I received a phone call from Anna's mum, who explained that she had gone down to the local shopping centre to have Anna's eyes tested. However, Anna had different ideas, and refused to allow the optician to test her eyes. She was adamant that she did not want glasses and nothing Anna's mum or the optician said would get Anna to sit in the optician's chair. I asked Anna's mum if she would let me have a go, and asked her to book another appointment for Anna for the following week.

Between that phone call and the appointment, I spent time with Anna. We did drawing and colouring in, and at every opportunity we added glasses to the people in the picture. We looked up photos of celebrities who wore glasses, and picked out our favourites. I enthusiastically spoke about how wearing glasses was 'cool' and, on the day of the appointment, brought a teddy with me who was wearing his own set of glasses.

By the time we arrived at the appointment, Anna was happy to sit in the optician's chair and excited by the prospect of being able to pick out some cool glasses once the eye test was over. As the eye test progressed, I reflected on this having been a successful piece of work and looked forward to reporting the good news to Anna's mum and dad. That moment didn't last long. With a smile on his face, the optician reported the good news – Anna didn't need glasses. Unfortunately, Anna didn't think this was such good news. I had so effectively convinced her on the 'coolness' of wearing glasses that Anna was now disappointed and upset that she didn't have to wear them! Thinking on my feet I was able to obtain some old glasses frames from the optician, and Anna happily went away with some lens-less but nevertheless 'cool' glasses.

Activity: When I'm Better
Purpose

- To help children look forward to what they can do once feeling better (optimism about the future and having things to look forward to and aim for can help children in their recovery).

What you will need

- large piece of blank paper (around A3 size)

- smaller pieces of paper

- good-quality felt tip pens

- Blu-tack™ or glue

- a photo of the child (optional).

What to do

1. With the child draw a picture of their house on the large piece of paper. Explain that rainbows represent hope. For younger children give an example of what hope is, for example, 'I hope that I get lots of presents for my birthday.' Then draw a rainbow going over the house.

2. As you are drawing and colouring these in with the child, explain that together you are going to plan out what the child will do once well enough/discharged from hospital. For

a child who may not be going home for a while, you might have to amend this activity and choose the next step in their journey as the goal. For example, if a child is in isolation and not allowed to leave the room/have visitors, the goal might be when they are no longer in isolation.

3. If in hospital and you have a date planned for discharge (and if this is a certainty), write the date at the bottom of the rainbow. Then put the photo of the child in the middle of the house.

4. Using the small pieces of paper, encourage the child to think about what they are looking forward to doing when their goal is reached; for example, they are able to go home. If some of these activities may not be possible due to the health of the child or for other reasons, acknowledge that some of the activities might take a long time to achieve. In such cases, you might suggest that you keep the goal, but also have another that is similar and could happen sooner; for example, going to the cinema might be the longer-term goal, with the other being having a friend over for a movie night, complete with popcorn. Invite them to draw these activities on the small pieces of paper.

5. Using the Blu-tack™ or glue, put the small drawings of activities on the rainbow.

6. Agree with the child where you will put up this drawing. Ideally this will be somewhere they can see it, so that when they are not feeling well or are discouraged they can look at this and remember what they are looking forward to. When the activities happen, they can be moved from the rainbow and put beside the child.

Activity: Road to Recovery
Purpose

•   To help the child to understand their care plan/the steps they need to go through in order to go home from hospital.

•   To support the child to have a visual record of the progress they have made.

What you will need

- large piece of paper (A3 or larger)
- good-quality felt tip pens
- smaller piece of paper
- craft materials (optional).

What to do

1. On one side of the large piece of paper, get the child to draw a picture of the hospital where the child is. On the other side of the paper, get the child to draw a picture of their house.

2. Explain to the child that in order to get from the hospital to the house we need to have a path or a road to join the two. With the child, draw a pathway or road connecting the two places. Lining the road should be a number of 'milestones', which can be represented however you wish. You might have trees, traffic lights or roundabouts. The number of 'milestones' you have will be the same as the number of actions/things that have to happen before the child can go home.

3. Next, using the smaller piece of paper or craft materials, ask the child to draw either a picture of themselves or make a model person to represent them. If drawing a picture of themselves, you want to be able to cut this out and place it on the road/pathway.

4. Inside each 'milestone' (e.g. a tree), write what needs to happen. Ensure that these are concrete and represent what is actually being measured, for example, rather than write 'when the cast is off', you might write 'when I can walk unaided'; rather than write 'when my parent can administer injections', you might write 'when my blood sugars are stable'. If the milestones are not necessarily going to happen in a particular order, then at step 2 above, you may want to draw each milestone picture separately and then stick them on, so that they can be removed once achieved.

5. Explain to the child as you write what each milestone involves and answer any questions they might have about them. The

picture can then be put up somewhere, and the figure of the child can be moved along each time another milestone is achieved. Be mindful that at times additional milestones may crop up that are unforeseen at the time of making the drawing, or the child might have to move backward again; for example, if blood sugars were stable but then become unstable again. You will want to prepare the child for this, if this is a possibility, as you work through the milestones.

An alternative to this would be to create a cartoon for/with the child that sequences the order of what has to happen. An example might be a picture for each of the following: to travel to the hospital, to be admitted to a ward, to see the doctor, to have an operation, to spend time in another ward whilst getting better, to then go back to the first ward, to then be told by the doctor you can go home, to go home. Again, you would make a figure or drawing of the child (and possibly the parent) and then move this along the cartoon timeline for each stage of the journey. You could encourage the child to add speech bubbles and thoughts at each stage they read in order to explore how they are feeling.

Activity: Bags of Stones (this will not be suitable for children who are developmentally younger)
Purpose

- To help the child who needs to make a decision about their care or treatment.

- To help a child to consider all the factors that might be present and their degrees of importance.

What you will need

- real stones or papier-mâché stones

- two bags, with 'advantage' or 'positive' written on one, and 'disadvantage' or 'negative' written on the other

- small pieces of paper and elastic bands, if using real stones

- pens.

What to do

1. Explain to the child that sometimes when there is a big decision to make it can be hard to decide what to do. Show the bags to the child and the stones, and explain that these can help in making a decision.

2. Give the child an example that is relevant to their interests. Keep it quite simple. An example might be that you know a little boy called John who is trying to decide whether to join a football club after school on a Friday. Picking up a stone explain that John says that he wants to go to football a lot so he gives it a score of 'eight out of ten'. Write eight on the stone and put it in the bag saying 'positive' or 'advantage'. Then pick up another stone and explain that John will miss playing out with his friend Robert if he goes to football, and that this is a negative. Explain that he gives this a score of 'six out of ten'. Having written six on the stone, put it in the other bag, which says 'negative' or 'disadvantage'. Explain that the bag with the most points is the one containing the football choice, and so this is the choice that Robert decides he will go for.

3. Next introduce the decision that the child is having to make. With the child, write on each stone (for real stones you will need to put this on paper and then wrap it round the stone with the elastic band) the advantages and disadvantages associated with that decision. You might also suggest some if the child is missing out what might be an important one. However, the decision to include it or not should be the child's. So, if the decision is about having an operation, an advantage might be that the child will be able walk better after, and a disadvantage might be that they will have pain for a few days after the operation.

4. Once all the advantages and disadvantages have been written, go through each one and ask the child to give it a scoring out of ten as to how important this is to them, For example, walking better might be worth seven points but having pain might be worth eight. Be mindful not to lead the children or influence them. Whilst we may have a particular view, this is about the child's viewpoint rather than ours.

5. As you score the stones, write on them and ask the child to place the stone either in the 'advantage/positive' bag or 'disadvantage/negative' bag depending on where it fits.

6. Once all the stones have been placed, look through what stones are on what side. Are there other stones that need to be added? Which of the stones have been given the most weighting?

7. Finally, add up the total number of points each bag has. Explore this with the child. Are they surprised by the outcome? Does this help them make a decision?

Siblings of children with serious illnesses

There are some specific things to consider with children who have a sibling who is unwell. As with any family illness, let the child know that they haven't caused their sibling to be unwell. The author's experience of working with siblings of children with serious illness is that they can experience a range of difficult and often conflicting emotions, and can then feel shame for feeling these emotions. As a result, it is important to have an awareness that some or all of the following emotions may be present for these children.

Jealousy

Children can feel jealous of the unwell sibling for the attention that they see their sibling getting, both from family members and also other adults. Parents and carers may spend time in hospital with the unwell child, meaning that they are physically (and potentially emotionally) less available for the child who isn't ill.

Guilt

The child may feel guilty that they are not the one who is unwell, and feel very sorry for their ill sibling. At the same time, if they also feel jealous of the attention that their unwell sibling is getting, they may then also feel guilt for having this emotion.

Rejected

A child may also feel that they are not important any longer or unloved because of the time and attention given to the ill sibling. This might be further exacerbated by their day-to-day problems not being given as much attention as they normally would, because they are seen as trivial in the context of the sibling's illness. In addition, siblings may have to spend periods of time with alternative carers such as grandparents or friends, if the parent(s) is in hospital with the sick child.

The activity 'Emotions' could be helpful for children to explore how they feel about their sibling being unwell. You may wish to intentionally introduce the above feelings, perhaps with a statement such as, 'Sometimes the brothers and sisters of a child who is poorly can feel jealous/guilty/rejected, and that's okay. I wonder if you have had this feeling...can you tell me about it?' It is also useful to explicitly acknowledge that we can have lots of different emotions all at the same time.

The following are suggestions on what you might do to support the sibling of an ill child:

- If possible, have the new caregiver move into the child's home, rather than the child having to stay with the caregiver. This minimises change and promotes stability and security for the child.

- Have a regular link to the parent(s) who is with the ill child. This might be that the parent calls each day and/or texts at a particular time. Again, the predictability of when this will be will promote stability for the child. However, don't do this if it is felt that there may be occasions when this would not or could not be followed through, as this can create anxiety if it doesn't happen.

- The parent might arrange for there to be a small gift or note under the pillow of the child every day so that they wake up/go to bed with this. This communicates to the child that they are special, and that the parent(s) is holding the child in mind, even when physically absent.

- If you know how long a parent will be away for, you could have an advent calendar with a message to the child behind each door, the number of doors counting down until the parent returns.

- If the child is staying outside their normal home environment, ensure they have significant items with them and, as much as possible, keep to the same routine. Reassure the child about what is happening to family pets or where other siblings are living if they are not with the child.

- Put in a routine for the child with regard to visiting the hospital, and as much as possible promote consistency in when they visit, who will take them, pick them up, etc.

- Ensure that the child has one-to-one time with the parent(s) who is staying with the ill child and that they know with certainty when that will be.

- Give the child a special job/role to do in relation to the sibling. The aim is to give a proportionate amount of responsibility, to allow the sibling to feel important and included – this also provides a safe opportunity for the sibling to express anger. One child I worked with was in charge of their unwell sibling's sunflower. She deliberately didn't water the flower and destroyed it, expressing her anger and frustration.

Remember that it is important for the sibling of the unwell child to have a full understanding of what is happening. Whilst a lot of thought may be given to how to speak to the unwell child, and this may be supported greatly by medical professionals, the siblings may miss out on this. They are likely to also pick up on adult conversations, yet may not have been given as much information as the child who is unwell.

Children will need to be supported at school and it is essential therefore that education staff are aware of what is happening for the child's family. It will be helpful for the child to know what they can do/who they can go to if they need some emotional support within the school day. Also, be aware that children may get bullied in relation to their sibling being unwell, particularly if the sibling has a disability that is obvious to peers.

Chapter 15

Talking to Children About Death and/or Suicide

Any death within the family is a difficult and painful experience for everyone. It is only natural that adults therefore want to protect children as much as possible from this pain; this is perhaps especially the case when a family member commits suicide. This chapter considers how to talk to children about death, including when this is by suicide.

In relation to mental health and suicide, there is much stigma in society, and many adults find it hard to talk openly about it. I (Audrey) recall some years ago that a colleague's brother had committed suicide. On her return to work I approached her and said that I was very sorry to hear about her brother's suicide and offered to be there if she needed me. My colleague burst into tears, at which point I started to apologise, fearing that I had been too direct. Instead my colleague explained that she was crying in relief that she had found someone who understood her: 'You are the first person who has said "suicide". And that's what he did and I need to talk about.'

Children need to hear the truth no matter how the person has died, and like my colleague they need to be given permission to talk about what has happened, as painful as that is for both them and the adults around them. Many people don't know how to tell the child, what words to use and how to say it. People also fear that the situation will be made worse if they are unable to cope with the child's reaction or have no answers to a child's questions.

One of the obstacles in talking to children about suicide is the fear that children will face some of the same questions that the adults might be facing: 'Was it my fault?', 'Why did they do that?', 'Could I have stopped them?' and 'Did it hurt?'

Despite all these reasons, adults can feel that they need to soften (or 'sugarcoat') the information when a person has died (particularly if by suicide). Yet this is in fact a misguided action that can lead to unintentional harm. I have listed below some of the difficulties that arise from not giving children the information they need.

1. Children are very tuned in, not only to the important people in their lives but also to the activity around them. Think of it as an inbuilt survival skill. Children generally just know if adults are hiding something from them or if there is something wrong. This usually creates anxiety, sometimes fear, and it is a common reaction for children to fill in the perceived gaps with their own explanations. These explanations, unfortunately, can be just as upsetting as the truth. Children are likely to blame themselves and, if they are unable to talk freely about what has happened, there is no opportunity for adults to comfort and reassure.

2. In the long term, in order to learn to accept a death, the child needs a coherent understanding of what has happened.

3. Children have 'big ears' and it is highly likely that they will overhear and attempt to interpret adult conversation and actions, but not fully understand what they hear. This is particularly the case around periods of stress, when children will pick up on the atmosphere and likely find ways of listening in. It is almost impossible to think that this will not happen after a death, particularly suicide, as it is often accompanied by many visits from family, friends and professionals. Children who have heard snippets of information and formed their own understanding of what has happened from conversations then have no way of talking about this as they have not been officially told.

4. Communities talk and, sadly, a suicide in the community is usually a newsworthy event. Other children will hear parts of conversations and can often be cruel to each other. I once had a situation where a 7-year-old child, Derek, was being bullied by another child of the same age. This child was chanting 'Your mum committed suicide, ha ha.' When I spoke to the child about what he was saying, I explained

that this was an unkind thing to do, especially as Derek was sad at the moment. The child asked why Derek was sad. It became clear that the boy did not know what it meant that Derek's mother had committed suicide, but that he had heard other people saying this. Once this had been explained to the boy, he apologised to Derek and asked to be his friend. This example highlights the significant risk that the child will either be told directly about the suicide by the community, or will hear whispers of it.

Given the above, it is clear that is always better for a child to hear such difficult and sad news from a person who they know and trust, so they are given accurate information in a way that is caring, supportive and appropriate for their stage of development. Being told in this way conveys the message that it is okay to talk about the person who has died, and about their death.

But how do you do this?

First, consideration needs to be given to who is best placed to tell the child. It is usually most appropriate for a close family member to do this, but given that the close family are likely to be grieving, they may need support. What this support looks like will be as individual as the people involved. However, it is often helpful to talk through words that could be used and to think about how to answer anticipated questions. It is often helpful to have another safe and helping adult to either take over or support once the initial telling of the information has been done. This is because it is not uncommon for the adult who has done the telling to experience a wave of distress, and need a break from being the focus of the child. In such cases, it is best for the adult who gave the information to stay with the child, but this does not preclude another safe and helping adult being there to answer questions and to offer emotional support to both parties. For some it is more helpful if the child is told the news on a one-to-one basis and, following this, the safe and helping adult joins the child and telling adult. This gives the possibility of the child being able to tell the joining adult what has happened, which can be empowering for them, or that the telling adult repeats the news to the safe and helping adult. In both situations, the child is able to affirm the information they have just received and receive additional care from a second party.

What do I say? How do I explain?

The first thing that the child needs to know is that the person has died. The child needs to be able to understand this and process what this means. When there has been a suicide, the fact that the person has died will need to be explained before helping the child to understand the concept of suicide. When telling a child that someone has died, it is important to use clear language. We suggest that you might say something like 'I have something very sad to tell you [pause]. Your mummy has died.' You may add 'Her body has stopped working' depending on the developmental stage of the child. It is crucial that you do not use phrases that can leave a child unclear or anxious. For example, 'Mummy has gone to sleep forever and won't wake up again' can lead children to fear that they or others may also go to sleep at night and not wake up again. An explanation of 'Mummy has gone to live in heaven' is also confusing. One boy whom I worked with had been given this explanation and asked me to take him to heaven, as this is where his mummy lived. He had not been taken to the funeral and had no sense of what death was. This led to a lot of painful and difficult work: his mother had died over a year ago and for that period of time he had believed that his mother had abandoned him and moved house. Once a child has understood that the person has died and what this means, it would then be appropriate, if relevant to the family, to speak about heaven or the place that the family believe to be the afterlife. Such an explanation may then bring comfort and a sense of closure. So the rule is keep to true and few words.

It is also very important at the point of telling a child of a death, to also tell them what will happen in a specific way. This is particularly the case if the person who has died was a primary or significant caregiver. For example, 'Granny will be looking after you now. She will do all the things that Mummy did, such as making you breakfast and taking you to school, giving you cuddles and finding teddy when he gets stuck under the bed. Aunty May will take care of you when Granny is at work. Granny loves you and Aunty May loves you.' When making such a statement, you need to include both practical and emotional care, and ensure that what you say is child-centred. This will also need to address any specific issues for the child; for example, a child who cannot sleep without their teddy needs to know who will ensure that they have the teddy.

What you say next very much depends on the child. Some children will ask questions immediately. It is best to answer questions as they arise, giving small chunks of information, letting the child dictate the pace and the amount of information they receive at any one time. If no questions arise, don't immediately jump in and give all the information at once. This can be tempting because as adults we can want to get it over with. Whilst that may be easier for us, it is rarely helpful for a child. Wait a while, and then at a later point in the day or the following day ask the child if they have any questions about the person who died. Some children need time to process, and that can include them needing to go and play.

If the child continues to not discuss the person who has died or ask any questions, a further opportunity needs to be offered by the adult using a gentle prompt. This should start with a simple open-ended question. For younger children, this may be posed by their favourite toy ('I was wondering how you are feeling'), or by inviting the child to do something to remember the person (e.g. 'I was going to draw a picture of your mummy dancing because I am missing her. Would you like to come and draw?'). Prompts such as these should give you the opportunity to move to the second stage that is required with a suicide, which is to give the child the specific information that the person died by committing suicide.

Explaining suicide

How you do this will depend on the child's developmental stage and their understanding of the person's mental health prior to death. It is important not to assume that a child understands the meaning of the word suicide. It is often better to give a simple but truthful account of what happened. The primary carer needs to lead in deciding what explanation is to be given. They may want some guidance and support in this, having decided how to explain to the child what will be said. Everyone around the child needs to ensure that they give the child the same explanation.

A lot of children have a knowledge of, or are able to understand the concept of people dying because a part of their body has stopped working. When this is the case, it can be helpful to explain suicide as something that happens in relation to the person's brain not working properly. If the child already has an awareness of the person having had mental ill health, then this could also be referred to.

Depression, for example, can be described in terms of the behaviours that it caused, such as 'Mummy feeling sad and crying a lot'. For older children, the allegory of a 'dark cloud' over that person may help. The child can be helped to understand that this illness also meant that 'Mummy's brain wasn't working properly and she believed that the only thing she could do was to kill herself to make the sadness and crying (or the dark cloud) go away.' One parent I worked with, when describing a hanging, explained to the child that 'Dad put a rope around his neck, and the rope stopped him getting enough air to breathe so he died.' This courageous and factual statement protected the young child from the graphic detail but gave him enough information to understand what had happened. It is anticipated that as he grows up he will have questions. However, sharing this with him at the time of his father's suicide has allowed him to trust that he will be told the truth and that it is okay to talk about his father's death. This in turn gives him the best possible chance of grieving in a healthy way.

Blame

Regardless of the cause of death, children will often think that it is their fault, particularly if it is a parent who has died. It therefore goes without saying that children should be reassured again and again that it is not their fault, and gently encouraged to talk about their feelings.

One 17-year-old I knew had blamed herself for her father's death. He had died of a massive heart attack having given her a lift to college that morning. She had been running late and pleaded with her father to take her. He had, but it meant that he had rushed around. She believed that if she had not put him under the added pressure, then he may not have died.

A 7-year-old girl told me that her grandfather would not have died if she had been good and picked up all her toys. Exploring this further, I found out that her grandad had often said to her, 'You'll be the death of me' when he tripped over a toy.

Funerals

It is not uncommon for adults to decide that children should not attend funerals, often because they feel protective. However, in my experience it can be very helpful for a child to be included in the funeral arrangement and to attend at least part of the funeral. It offers them a shared experience and can help with the grief process in a similar way to how it helps adults. Helping the child to make something to give at the funeral or giving a child a role to play can help them to feel part of this. This might include the child making a daisy chain to place on the coffin, the child choosing a picture or a hymn or song to be incorporated, the child helping to bake for the wake, writing a poem or choosing flowers.

It is okay for children to see adults crying and being upset, as this gives permission for the child to do the same.

It is helpful for the child to have a named special person at the funeral, whether that is a best friend's parent, an extended family member or a neighbour. This should be someone who the child trusts and likes, and regularly spends time with. The purpose of this is to have someone solely dedicated to meeting that child's needs at a time when those who normally would do this may be distracted by their own grief. The named special adult should be able to leave with the child whenever they wish or when the adult judges that they need to, either for some short respite such as by going out to kick a ball around, or to leave and go home.

Talking and remembering

It perhaps seems obvious that talking about and remembering a loved one is a positive thing to do. However, sometimes families struggle to know how to do this; people worry about upsetting each other and sometimes there is an ethos of 'keep busy and don't talk' as a way of coping.

The following are activities to support talking and remembering:

Activity: Rainbow Memories
Purpose

- To create an opportunity to prompt memories, to talk about and record these.

What you will need

- A rainbow – there are several options for this. I have a beautiful wooden rainbow that I sit on the table with bits of card in the rainbow's colours to write on. Older children will possibly prefer this option. Or you can provide a large piece of paper (I like to use lining paper) and use poster paints in order to create a rainbow, for memories to be written onto. In both cases, it is also good to have photographs of rainbows available. You may also decide to use any other items that are relevant, such as crystals (or any form of dispersive prism) that will cast a rainbow, and you could even make some rainbow jelly as a snack.

What to do

1. Explain to the child that rainbows are very special, and are a symbol of hope for many. You can explain that in some cultures people view then as a bridge from earth to heaven, and others believe that they have magical qualities. Most children like rainbows and you can look at the photos of rainbows and choose a favourite, ask them what their favourite colour is and whether they have seen a real rainbow. You might also ask them what they think about rainbows.

2. Then explain that rainbows can help us to remember people or special occasions. Give an example, such as that the red of the rainbow makes you think of Christmas because Santa's coat is red and there is lots of red around Christmas. You might give a specific memory personal to you. So, for example, I might explain that my dad has now died but that I remember him taking us to cut a Christmas tree down at Christmas, or remember that when he worked in the garden a robin red breast used to come and sit on the spade really close to him. Try to give your own example that is real,

but at the same time respect where your own boundaries lie. By giving more than one memory for a colour you can demonstrate that children can have lots of memories for each colour. You then ask the child whether they have any 'red' memories for the person who has died.

3. Next, and with enthusiasm, suggest that you make a rainbow and talk about your memories of the person as you do it. Suggest that as you chat about it, you can write the memories down or draw the memories onto the rainbow. Lots of children I work with find writing hard work, so I will offer to do the writing.

Extension activity

Depending on the interests of the child, you may want to provide beads in rainbow colours so that you can make a rainbow memory bracelet or mosaic pieces in rainbow colours to decorate a plant pot. This can be done at the end of the session as a way of winding down from what may have been a very emotional session. It also provides a transitional object for the child to take with them that is not overtly about the grieving/remembering process. The child should be asked if they want to take their memory rainbows away with them. Some children will want to, and will want to share these openly, whilst others will want to take them away but put them in a safe place and take them out from time to time. Others will want you to keep them safe. Go with what the child wants to do. If they want you to keep the work, check whether they want someone to look at it first, and also discuss with them and their carer what will happen to this work when your working relationship ends.

Activity: Memory Jar
Purpose

*   To provide an activity that records memories, as an ongoing process that everybody who visits the home can be invited to help/join in with. This then offers a shared memory bank and opportunities to reflect. This activity can help people to feel supported by their family, friends and possibly the wider community.

What you will need

- a big jar – you can get these from traditional sweet shops, who will usually give you their empty jars free of charge

- plain index cards

- ribbons, stickers, etc. to decorate the jar

- glue and scissors.

What to do

1. Decorate the jar! Let the children do whatever they wish. It might be helpful to have the colour or pictures of things that the deceased person liked. Or, if you don't know, have a wide variety of choices. One sibling group I worked with covered the whole jar in pink tissue and then on top of this had photos of their mum and stickers of dogs, as she had loved dogs. On the other hand, a young man I worked with simply tied a ribbon around the neck of the jar with a homemade label that said 'Memories of Dad'.

2. Now give everyone an index card and ask them to write or draw a memory on the card and place this in the jar. If you knew the deceased, you could also join in. People can use as many index cards as they wish. The only rule is that they only put one memory on each card. This is because you want to fill the jar and also because each individual memory is important. When others visit the family they can be invited to add a memory, that is, fill in an index card.

3. The family as a whole or as individuals can review the cards when they wish. The jar should be placed somewhere that can be easily accessed. Some families place it in a prominent place, such as above the fireplace, whilst others prefer a private place. As people work through the grief process they may want to move the jar; or some family members may want it in clear view with others wanting to hide it away. I would suggest a compromise is that it is placed in clear view but in a space where people will not spend long periods of time; for example, the hallway.

PRACTICE EXAMPLE

Having been working with a father and son, I explained to the father one day how to make a memory jar and provided him with the materials. I gave him some space to explore his own feelings and he decided that he would make the jar with his son on a Friday evening. I agreed that I would check in with him after the weekend to see how things had gone. On arriving at the home on Monday I was met by a very emotional father. He explained that he and his son had made the jar on Friday as planned and that it had gone as he had expected it to. They had placed the jar on a shelf in the living room, but in a place that his 9-year-old son could reach.

On Saturday, the son went out to play but was away a bit longer than normal. When his father looked outside the house he couldn't see him so, getting worried, he went out to look for him. However, he was unable to find him, and was at the point of calling the police when his son arrived home. His son had a serious look on his face, and greeted his father saying, 'I've got the memory jar full, Dad. In fact, I think we need to make another one!' The son had gone to every house on the street, to the local shops where his mum had done her shopping and to the community centre, and invited everyone to add a memory. Each person had obliged and, as a result, there were many precious memories in the jar. And perhaps more importantly, the father and son felt supported by their local community.

Activity: Treasure Box

Purpose

- A place to keep special things that remind you of the person.

What you will need

- shoe box

- sticky back plastic (comes in many colours and patterns and can be bought from craft stores – used to cover the box as well as strengthening it)

- things to decorate the box

- scissors

- a few pieces of treasure to start with, for example, a photo of the deceased person, an item of their clothing such as a scarf, the order of service from the funeral, etc.

What to do

1. Explain to the child that it can be good to have a special place to keep precious things or treasure that might help them to remember the person who died.

2. Show them the items that you have already gathered – if at all possible get items that target all the senses; for example, a photo for sight, clothing to touch, a piece of their favourite music to hear, a perfume the person wore to smell and a favourite snack to taste (this will obviously need replacing regularly).

3. Show the child the box and invite them to pick what they want to decorate it with. If you are working with a child who is under 12, I would suggest that you cover the box in a natural colour of sticky back plastic before you start. It is tricky stuff to use and so takes time – younger children are likely to be frustrated and bored by the time it takes. However, because it strengthens the box it is worth doing.

4. As the child decorates the box, use lots of affirming statements but also invite conversation about the person you are remembering.

5. When the box is finished, fill it (invite them to add any other items to the box that they can think of), admire it, maybe take a photo of it and help the child to decide where they are going to keep it.

PRACTICE EXAMPLE

Having made a treasure box with a parent and her two children aged 8 and 12, I realised that we had limited access to items to put in it. I had sourced a photo and a scarf, and Mum provided Dad's favourite snack and aftershave. I was worried that I had perhaps started an activity that could end up causing upset. However, I decided (with parental permission) to contact the extended family, who at that time had limited contact with my young clients, to ask for their help. This had to be done with a great deal of sensitivity because, clearly, they were also grieving. I was careful to be humble in my explanation, stating that I had been trying to help but had not realised that the parent and children had very little to put in the box, and had very limited contact with the deceased parent's family. Not all, but most of the relatives I approached, wanted to help. They provided items and expressed a wish to include the children in their lives – this resulted in the children gaining a huge amount of immediate support and in the long term they went on holidays with their extended family.

It is important I think to forgive ourselves when we make potential mistakes and to realise that it is not the mistakes that are the biggest concerns, but rather what we do with them. In my experience, you often get a different but positive outcome.

Activity: Stones

Purpose

- To stimulate talk about both positive and difficult memories.

- Giving permission to remember the difficult memories is important as it helps to keep things realistic.

What you will need

- a smooth stone, for example, a stone from a river or one that you would place as a decoration on top of soil on plant pots

- a rough stone, for example a red chip from a driveway

- a special stone, for example a semi-precious stone such as rose quartz

- (You may want two or three of each stone.)

- a tiny drawstring bag (you can easily make one) or a covered box.

What to do

1. Place the stones in the bag or the box and explain that there are all different kinds of memories, and that you have some stones to help you with the different memories.

2. Give the child the bag/box, and invite them to look inside. Explain that you think that the smooth stone would help you remember ordinary kinds of memories that went smoothly, such as watching a film together, and ask the child what they think. Then explain that the rough stone would help you to remember something hard or a difficult time, and that the special stone might remind you of a very precious or special memory.

3. Pop all the stones back into the bag and ask the child to pick one out and talk about that kind of memory. You may wish to record these memories for the child on a thin piece of paper and then wrap that piece of paper around each stone. The child can then take their wrapped-up stones away in the bag or box and refer back to them as they wish.

Activity: Candle Work
Purpose

- To identify the important people in a child's life and to help the child to feel valued and connected to people.

What you will need

- tealight candles (I buy a big value-bag of white ones)

- tealight candles in different colours (as many as possible)

- matches

- tin foil or recycled foil trays

- a steady table – cover it in tin foil or lay the trays on it

- a space without a smoke alarm and that is not too draughty (this is the biggest challenge!)

- if working with a very young child, or a child who is very active or has a conduct disorder, you will need another adult who has a good relationship with the child to help you keep this activity safe.

What to do

1. Take your candle tin (I use an old biscuit tin) out of your bag and explain to the child that you are going to do something really fun and exciting. Play a guessing game with the child – can the child guess what is in the box? You might give the child clues to guess. Most people are fascinated by or enjoy candles, and for children and young people there is a sense of being allowed to do something fun and a little bit risky, which adds to the attraction. Having this kind of introduction to the activity gives an opportunity to set the tone of the session as upbeat, positive and fun.

2. Once you have opened the box or tin, explain that you are going to light lots of candles, so many in fact that the room is going to glow and be cosy and warm. Ask the child to help you get the space ready. Put the tin foil over the table or lay baking trays out. Whilst doing this, I talk to the child about trust. I emphasise that I only do this with children whom I can trust to listen, to be sensible and safe. We push up long sleeves, and tie back long hair. I like to ask everyone who is participating to wash their hands (and possibly wipe their face) before we start. You don't have to do this, but I feel it adds to the importance of the occasion and helps the child to feel refreshed and focused.

3. To begin, I ask the child to choose a favourite candle to represent themselves. I offer a choice from the coloured candles,

some of which will also have patterns. They may not be tealight candles but they are always small. We place that candle in the centre of the table, admire it and talk about for a few minutes. We might talk about why it was the child's favourite, or a time when the child remembers a candle. Then I invite the child to choose another special candle to represent someone in their life who is special/important to them. We then decide where we will place it in relation to the candle representing the child. Very close perhaps? We repeat the process of talking about the candle and the person it was chosen for. Repeat this process until all the child's important people have a candle on the table. Stay child-centred if the child names someone as an important person in their life but you don't think that is accurate. Be curious but don't disagree. One teenage boy I was working with told me he chose a special candle 'for this bloke I once met. I dinnae ken his name but he was cool'. I asked why he was special. He stated, 'He telt me ma mother was wrang for battering me and gave me money for a sweet. I was just wee.'

4. Once all the special people have been named, move to use the white candles. Ask the child to light a candle for everybody who knows him or her. In my experience, you will run out of candles before you run out of people, and that is just what you want to happen. Celebrate with the child all the people that they know, and how important they are to these people.

5. Having all the candles burning is a wonderful sight. Encourage the child to enjoy it and emphasise that the child has made it happen by having so many people in their life. Stand back from the table and stretch your arms out. Ask the child if they can feel the soft warm heat. Suggest that this is maybe like friendship – comforting and good. Walk as far away from the candles as you can. You can still see them, so even when they are far away, friends and important people are still there. Ask the child if they can picture the candles in their head? Can the child picture their important person (or the person who has died)? Suggest that though that person is not here today (the person who has died), they are always with

the child. Tell the child that the next time they feel lonely or are in trouble, they could remember all the candles, then choose one of their important people to remember. They could then think about what that person would do with the child if they were there, or what they would say about things. This part is more suited to older children, but can be done with younger children, depending on their development. A child of 4 whose mother had died announced to her nursery nurse after I had done this exercise with her, 'My mummy's a star now but she is in my head too. I can see her anytime!'

6.   Lastly, I take a photograph and then we blow out the candles and tidy up. Some children might find this bit hard so it is important to remind them that, even when the candles are not lit, they can remember all the people. I might ask the carer of the child to keep a special candle for the child, which they can light together, when needed.

Follow up

Get the photograph developed quickly and make a nice frame for it with the child or stick it onto card. Let the child decorate the card and then laminate it.

Activity: Message Balloons

Purpose

- To initiate conversation around what we would say to the person who has died (can also be used for a person who is missing, is in prison or is no longer seen following adoption).

What you will need

- balloons, or if you prefer, paper Chinese lanterns

- pens

- a quiet outdoor area

- a story about the wind taking messages (optional).

What to do

1. Have a conversation about what the child (and perhaps you too) would like to say to the absent person. Suggest that maybe the wind could carry this message to the person.

2. Write or draw the message on the balloon and then send it off by either just letting it go, or tying a string on the end and releasing it when the wind tugs at it. Ask the child which way they would prefer to do it.

PRACTICE EXAMPLE

I was privileged to work with a family where sadly the gran had died. The gran and grandad were the main caregivers for their grandchildren, and had been for the previous 3 years. The grandad was a proud man, and with four children under 12 to care for, he became highly organised in order to cope with all the practical care tasks. Fairly rigid routines were put in place and, on a practical level, this worked very well as it meant that the children received good physical care, went to school regularly and accessed a variety of clubs and groups. However, he himself recognised that there was 'never time to talk about their gran'. He worried that he would raise the subject at the wrong time for one of the children.

Through discussion, Grandad identified that he would like to make a corner of the garden into a remembrance garden for himself and the children, and agreed that the children should take part if they wished. The grandad asked for my support to tell the children and so I brought with me paper, pens, glue and craft items. I spoke to the children about the ideas and suggested that the children make models of what they would like Gran's garden to be like. They were all enthusiastic and this naturally facilitated talking about their gran: 'We have to have pink flowers as that was Gran's favourite colour', 'Can we get a gnome because she thought that they were funny?', 'We will need a seat so we can sit and think.'

Following this planning, every Saturday morning, Grandad worked on the garden with the children helping. I suggested that mid-morning, Grandad provided a snack and instigate conversation around Gran to support this. I suggested he start a sentence with 'I remember when' in order to indicate to the children that he was about to share a memory of their gran. This also opened up the opportunity for the children to share memories. It was also made clear that the children did not have to help with the garden and sometimes they chose not to. However, they usually joined their grandad for a snack. This project was fairly long, and thus the children had a couple of months of organised opportunities to talk about and remember their gran. Grandad put a picnic table in the remembrance garden and they continued to have their Saturday snack at the table even after the project was concluded.

Chapter 16

Talking to Children About Giving Evidence in Court

Adults will usually find giving evidence in court a very difficult thing to do. Not only that but it is not something that the majority of adults will ever have to do. If this is true of yourself then we would suggest that it would be helpful to visit a court and learn about the experience, perhaps observing a court case in the public gallery prior to preparing the child.

Even for those practised at giving evidence, it can be a tough process, so we can appreciate that for a child it may be a very frightening experience. The child is being asked to talk about an event that is probably at best upsetting and at worst traumatic, which in itself is a difficult thing to do. Couple that with a strange environment, and the fact that the child won't know a lot of the people who speak to them, and it may seem surprising that children manage to give evidence at all. The level of stress and/or distress will depend on the child's stage of development, their personality, the nature of the evidence they are required to give and who the evidence is against. You need to know your child and keep consulting with them, working hard to find out from them what their fears as well as preferences are. You then need to work together to try and address these. That said, they will not know what they are going into, and so you will need an awareness of the common stress factors and the best way to support children through this process. This chapter aims to help you with that. However, the services available and the way the court works will vary from place to place, so this can only be a broad guide to point you in the right direction.

- Starting the conversation about going to court is usually relatively simple. As a starting point, the court will have sent a letter out advising that the child needs to attend to give evidence, and this can be how you raise the subject.

- It is important to be explicit about what 'going to court' and 'giving evidence' is. Don't assume that the child understands. Even if the child says that they understand, check out their understanding. One boy told me (Audrey) in his broad Scottish accent, 'Och, you just go and hae a wee chat wi' the sheriff mannie and then you gang for chips after' (Oh, you just speak to the judge man and then you go for chips after). This was how his father had described the court process, and had I accepted that he knew all about it, he would have been ill-prepared for giving evidence. I did, however, make sure we went for chips after!

- There are a number of relatively simple things that you can do to help. Perhaps the most important thing is to recognise that standing in a court room opposite the person you are giving evidence about, in a formal setting with lots of strangers, can be challenging for an adult to do. In our view, it is just too much to ask a child to do given the imbalance of power in any child–adult relationship, particularly when the person in question may have abused their trust and power. There are alternatives in place that you can ask for, such as children being able to give evidence from a remote location via video link, given that they would qualify as a 'vulnerable witness'. Part of your preparation with the child before giving evidence would be to visit this and see how it works. Contact the court as soon as you know the child is to give evidence, not only to book the remote location for the court date but also for a visit. In a lot of places there is only one remote location and the courts are often busy. If this facility is not available or not agreed to, then ask for screens to be provided. These go in front of the witness stand so the witness can just see the sheriff (judge). However, apart from the obvious fact that they are not as effective as giving evidence remotely, the person whom evidence is being given against may make subtle noises (such as a cough or a sigh) to remind the witness they are there. This can have a profound effect on the witness. Be aware that the child is able to have a support person with them to sit next to them. Again, make a point of visiting the court and seeing the screens in place, including standing in the witness box before the court date. Witness services can help you organise this. Whilst you will want to book the visits early on, you ideally want to visit nearer to the time of giving evidence to maintain a sense of familiarity.

- Remember to explain to the child the purpose of giving evidence. You might explain that the 'sheriff (judge) is very wise and wants to understand what happened. You need to help her by telling your true story'.

- Tell the child what will happen in detail, including who will take them, what they will see and what they will do. Use photographs of the court, and find photos of how the sheriff or judge will dress. There are also stories about going to court that are available for children. Witness services in your own area may have published leaflets about your local court, which will be helpful.

- Organise for the child to meet with the person who has called them and will lead evidence from them (in Scotland this is the procurator fiscal, who is the public prosecutor). This meeting should take place in a relaxed setting. Ask this person to not wear their gown but to bring a photo with them in their gown and to ensure that they wear their hair in the same way as they will have it in court. They may be able to wear the same clothes on the day of the court case and to not have to wear a gown – in essence, what you are trying to achieve is that the person looks familiar to the child. Sometimes people think that this is important only for younger children. However, the child may be developmentally younger and on the day is certainly going to be under stress and therefore not processing information as easily. This concession is, therefore, equally as important for an older child or a teenager as it is for a younger child. Prior to the meeting, you should, if at all possible, meet with the prosecutor and advise them of any words that the child uses for people or things that are likely to be used in the court, and ask them to use these words. For example, does the child refer to their mother as 'mum', 'mummy', 'mam' or something else? Again, this can ease a child's stress levels and aid them to give evidence because they are not trying to process unfamiliar language. You may also want to advise the prosecutor of the child's fears so that, if one of their fears is mentioned, the prosecutor will know this might upset the child. People who abuse children can be highly manipulative and may, for example, suggest to their lawyer that they question a child about a particular thing that they know will cause the child fear or upset. As well as advising of fears, it can be helpful to advise the prosecutor of a child's interests in order to support them to build rapport with the child.

- Explain to the child that if they do not understand a question then they should just say that, and that if they don't know the answer then it is okay to say 'I don't know.' Children may need help to understand that, unlike at school, they shouldn't be guessing the answers to questions. Ask the prosecutor to reiterate this information and assure the child that it is okay not to understand or not know the answer.

- Do explain to the child that the defence lawyer may appear to be cross or that the child might feel that they are not listening to them. Assure the child that this is just that lawyer doing their job.

- Reassure the child that they just need to tell their true story/tell the truth.

- Do explain that the outcome of court is not their responsibility – that it is the sheriff (judge) who decides.

- Reassure the child repeatedly that they are safe and name the people who keep them safe, and how they will do this. Encourage them to ask the 'what if…' questions if they have them. Try to help them explore their feelings, and that it is okay to feel scared/excited/mixed up/pleased/worried.

- Plan carefully for the day they give evidence. Identify a support person and also a second support person in case the first is ill.

Encourage the child to bring a comfort toy/item with them to have at all times. Think about clothing – this should be smart but comfortable and easy to get on or off when they go to the toilet. Prompt them to go to the toilet before giving evidence. Bring toys or electronic devices to entertain the child in the waiting room and a sandwich or snack. Try to avoid a lot of sugar as you don't want them to have excessive energy.

- Try to limit the amount of time that the child needs to wait before giving evidence. Speak to the court about this – most witnesses are required to arrive at the start of court. However, there is a long process to go through before witnesses are called. For child witnesses, I have found courts to be sympathetic and, if I am supporting a child, they will usually allow me to bring the child a bit later. This cuts down the time that they need to wait by a couple of hours.

- Do plan an activity for after the child has given evidence. You don't want this to be something that could be perceived as a bribe if it were talked about by the child in court, but something ordinary such as going to the local play park. It gives the child a way of understanding that the giving of evidence is just a part of their day. It also gives them something else to focus on and will provide an opportunity for them to let off steam or unwind afterwards.

- Don't tell the child what to say or practice what they are going to say. Don't bribe them into giving evidence, and don't tell them that their evidence will be the only thing that influences the outcome of court, even if that is true. It is just too much pressure.

PRACTICE EXAMPLE

Colin, aged 11, had to give evidence against a family member who had assaulted him. His brother Alex, aged 7, also had to give evidence.

I organised for the two brothers to give their evidence by video link at a remote location. We visited the location. It was just after the children had received the letter to say that they had to give evidence. Colin had become very worried about where he would have to go and I wanted to settle his fears as quickly as I could. A second visit was made 2 days before the children gave evidence so that on the day the place would feel familiar. In talking to Colin about what he felt would help, he advised that he needed two support people. He wanted me there because he saw me as a person who kept him safe and knew what was happening, and he wanted his grandfather there because he had previously been a boxer and 'was strong'.

We looked at photos of the local court and I brought some dressing up clothes – a robe and pretend wig that I had made from wool, toilet rolls and old towels! Alex enjoyed dressing up and we all had turns at playing the different roles. I left leaflets and a story book about going to court with their grandparents, asking them to go through these with the children.

Colin had a clear understanding of why he was going to give evidence: 'So as he [the perpetrator] can get the jail'. I was careful to ensure that all Colin could do was to tell the truth, and that the sheriff would decide about 'the jail' based on everything he or she heard. I explained to Colin that this would include what he said, but also what Alex said and what the police and other people said too. I wanted to try and ensure that if things did not go the way that Colin wanted, then he would not blame himself. Alex understood that he needed to go to the court to tell the sheriff about how he got hurt. He understood that the person who hurt him would get a consequence.

Both Colin and Alex needed a lot of reassurance that they would be safe. This included reassurance that no one would know where the remote location was, and the police would be able to get the perpetrator if he attempted to come and take the boys.

We planned carefully what they would wear and take with them, and what they wanted for a snack/picnic whilst waiting. I explained that they might have such a long wait that they would probably have time to watch a film. We planned that after the court we would go to the local park.

We also met the procurator fiscal (prosecutor) twice in a café before the court case. He ensured that he wore the same clothes on both of these occasions, and when he took evidence from the boys. I had met with him before he met with me and the children. He was therefore aware that Colin was concerned about the remote location being found. The procurator fiscal reassured Colin that it was a very secret place and that only professionals knew its location. It was very powerful for Colin to hear the same message from all the adults. The procurator fiscal was also aware that Alex was interested in dinosaurs and so he was ready to chat with him about the stegosaurus, which immediately interested Alex. The positive effect of getting to know the procurator fiscal was evident on the day, when the children both smiled on seeing him. He was able to chat with the children about 'being at work and that they were going to help him'. When the case had ended and the perpetrator received a prison sentence, the children made a card for the procurator fiscal to say thank you. This was instigated by Colin and I think highlights the importance of the procurator fiscal having built rapport with the children.

On the day itself, as well as bringing the film and some popcorn (requested by Alex), I also brought my small mobile sand tray, playdough, pens and paper, and marbles. The intention to watch a film was a good one, and it was important that I went with this as the children had chosen the activity, but I knew they would find it hard to concentrate and thus it would probably not work. On arrival, we settled into the small waiting room, which had its own integrated toilet. Once you are in, you are not allowed to leave. I decided not to point this out unless it came into conversation as I thought that this might upset the boys. The boys put the film on and we broke out the popcorn, but as predicted their nerves meant that concentration was poor. Both, in the end, used the sand and playdough. Activities that are sensory and allow fidgeting and movement often bring most comfort.

Both boys were able to give sound evidence that resulted in a conviction and prison sentence. This was down to their bravery, good preparation and collaborative working with the family and other professionals close to the boys (so that they felt safe and supported).

Chapter 17

Talking to Children About Imprisonment

As adults we will hold differing beliefs and views around offending. Particular crimes may bring up strong emotions. The majority of the population will not have been inside a police interview room or a prison, and many of us will have not been to court. As a result there is usually some fear or wariness, which is just a natural response to something that is unfamiliar and unknown.

It is, therefore, not surprising that talking to children about a close family member going to or being in prison, or having engaged in offending behaviour, can bring up difficult emotions and dilemmas over how to deal with the subject. This can be the case both for family and also for professionals.

It is not unusual for families to feel that the best thing is not to tell the child that an absent member of the family is in prison. I worked with one mother who told her 5-year-old daughter that her father was away at 'his work'. This became problematic when 5-year-old Stacey began to question why her dad didn't come home from work each night as her friends' fathers did. Further problems arose when she told the local shopkeeper that her daddy was at work; he laughed before replying, 'Well, that's good, never heard it called that before'. This left a rather confused child. We would always promote honesty with children. The important and trickier thing to consider is how to present the information, and how much information to give. There are no easy answers or blanket rules to apply, and this will depend on the child's developmental stage and their social experiences in terms of media, peer influence and exposure within the community. The wishes of the child's parents/main caregivers will also need to be respected. Professionals need to bear in mind that the child will spend relatively little time with them in comparison to their main caregiver, and it is likely therefore that the main caregiver will be the person who deals with questions.

In preparing to do the work:

1. The first step is to examine your own values, views and feelings. Be honest with yourself. You need to be aware of your own emotions as these can impact on how you engage with a child. Try to explore where your values and feelings are coming from. Professionals may have access to supervision as a place to explore this. If this is not the case, or for non-professionals, find a trusted colleague or friend to discuss this with.

2. Review and develop your knowledge. It is easier to have conversations, to guide and give advice about subjects when you have a good knowledge base. This might involve speaking to a police officer if this is something you can access. You could also visit the court and sit in the public gallery, to observe a few court cases and get a sense of how these run. You may also be able to make a general visit to the local prison, depending on your role. Many prisons have materials that have been designed for children, explaining the prison visiting process.

3. You will need to have a discussion with the main caregiver to the child. If this is not the parent, you must also take the parent's views into account. The main focus will be to find out from them what the child has been told or what they want the child to know. It is important to give people space to explore their own feelings and this is a good opportunity to do that: imprisonment affects not only the person in prison but also their friends and family. This can be on a practical level, for example, loss of income or loss of practical support, but can also be on an emotional level, such as through loss and change and/or the stigma of having a loved one in prison. Bear in mind that in some communities, the family may become isolated. Where there is resistance to being

honest with a child, it can be helpful to gently challenge this by helping people to see the potential difficulties that may arise from not being honest. I tend to use questions such as, 'So what would happen if…?' and 'Can you tell me what you would do if…?'

Having done the above preparation and reached an agreement with the parent(s) or main carer(s) as to what the child is going to be told, you need to think through the plan to actually tell the child. Perhaps the easiest way to do this is to consider the 'who', where', 'what', 'when' and 'why' questions.

Who

Who is going to tell the child? We would suggest that the best person to tell the child is the main carer, and that the worker's role would be to support the carer to do this, before, during and afterwards. The worker may also need to offer the child support and the opportunity to talk about this news, and what might be shocking and distressing information for them.

Where

Whilst at home might be an appropriate place, we would suggest that you avoid telling the child in their bedroom. The child's bedroom should be a place that they can retreat to, a place of comfort and safety. The living room or kitchen might be suitable, but you need somewhere quiet where there won't be interruption. Another place that can for some children be a good place for difficult conversations is the car. There is something comforting about the movement of a car and also the fact that direct eye contact is not required. You might choose to go somewhere with a short break built in, such as a trip out to buy ice cream. This gives the journey out to share the information, a chance for a break and then the journey home as a space for reflection and for questions to be asked. The drawback of using the car is that a child cannot leave the space or take a break easily. Be guided by the child's coping mechanisms as to what venue is best.

What

What is going to be said? It really is worth thinking this through and not just 'winging' it on the day. The language used and the explanation given need to be age- and stage-appropriate and, as much as possible, should mirror children's everyday language and understanding of the world. For example, children understand the concept of their unacceptable behaviour leading to consequences, and so you may choose to draw on this when explaining a custodial sentence.

Some examples

> Your mum made a choice to take lots of clothes from a shop without paying for them. That was wrong and so the sheriff [or judge] who is a very wise person, decided that the consequence for your mum would be to have adult 'time out' in a place called prison. This means that mum cannot live at home just now and cannot go to the shops. She has to stay inside the prison so she has time to think about her behaviour.

> Your dad hit me. It is not okay to hurt people so the sheriff [or judge], who is a wise person, said that your dad was not allowed to stay with us, and has to stay in prison just now.

> Uncle Jim used hurting hands. He was naughty so he is having calm down time in a place for grown-ups called prison.

> Aunty Lynn took a lot of money that did not belong to her so the sheriff [or judge] said that her consequence is that she has to live in prison until the summer.

Having given the child the basic facts, it is important to be ready for possible questions. It is also important to be able to provide reassurance and some additional information. The following are some of the questions and additional information that you may need to explore with the child.

What is prison?

If the child does not ask this question, the adult should sensitively create an opportunity to describe prison. Children may have some ideas about what prison is based on, either through television or from peers, and may believe that everything they have seen or heard is true. At best this is likely to be inaccurate and at worst may leave them frightened.

Think about how you will describe prison. Be honest but try to highlight the positives and to some extent normalise it, as children will usually be very loyal to adults whom they have had a relationship with. It is worth noting that this is not uncommon for children even when the adult in question has hurt them, especially if those adults have also met their needs on some level. Therefore, children are likely to be worried about the person in prison and concerned for them. Whilst remaining honest, the helping adult will want to try and alleviate this worry.

A suggested description of prison

It is a big building with a high fence around it. Lots of people are sent to live there for a while by the sheriff (or judge). The people who live in a prison are there as a consequence of their behaviour and are sometimes called 'prisoners'.

There are other people in the prison, too, who work there. There are nurses in case anyone gets sick or needs to take medicine each day, and a doctor can visit the prison when they are needed. There are social workers to help people with practical problems and to talk about any worries that people have. Social workers can also help the prisoners think about the reason that they have the consequence of being in prison and think about how they might do things differently once they go home. Social workers sometimes help the prisoner's family too. Then there is the governor and he or she is the 'big boss', a little bit like the head teacher at school. They have the job of making sure that everything is working well and that everyone stays safe. Then there are prison officers. They are there to look after the prisoners, but also to make sure that people behave and follow the rules, just like teachers at school.

The prison officers and governor are the only people who have the key for the door. They let people in and out of prison. [Member of family] can only leave when the sheriff [or judge] says that it is time. Then the prison officer will unlock the door and let them out.

Some prisons are for men and some are for women. Some prisons have men and women but they usually live in separate parts of the prison.

[Member of family] will share a small bedroom (in prison it is called a cell), usually with another prisoner, though some people have their own room. They will have breakfast, lunch and tea in a big dining hall where everyone eats together. During the day, [member of family] will be able to go to classes and learn new things – like school, or go to work inside the prison – maybe doing the washing or helping in the kitchen. Or they might just want to watch television or play a game, or read a book. They will be able to buy some small snacks or newspapers from a shop in the prison. We can leave a little money with one of the prison officers so that they can buy something nice.

One of the rules in prison is that [member of family] will not be allowed to have their own phone. This is just part of the consequence. There are phones that they can use when the prison officers say it is time. Sometimes there is a long queue of people wanting to use the phone and so that means that [member of family] can try to phone you but they might not get the chance if there are too many people in front of them before the time is up [obviously, you will say what is applicable having checked this out with the prison]. We are not able to phone [member of family] but we could write them a letter and I am sure that it would make them very happy to get this in the post.

Release date

It is important that the child knows that the person in prison is safe, but also that they cannot leave until they are released. Make sure you also let the child know that they will be told when the person is going to get out of prison.

There are several reasons for doing this. First, children cope best when things are predictable. Having a family member go into prison and come out of prison are both significant and life changing events that require emotional adjustment. Therefore, supporting children to get ready for this change by telling them in advance is important. Second, we should not assume that the family member being in prison is viewed as a negative thing by the child. Many children live with abusive family members for years without disclosing abuse. The period of time during which the family member is in prison may be providing respite. If this is the case, then advising the child of the release date (you would use 'coming home day' or 'so many sleeps until they are home') and asking the child how they might feel about this offers the child the chance to share both positive and negative emotions. Note that we are not making assumptions, so you wouldn't introduce a family member being released by saying 'I've got good news'. Asking how the child feels also helps the child to start thinking about what this change might mean for them. Some children use this time to disclose abuse they have experienced or witnessed. Third, up to now we have been writing on the basis that the person who has been convicted has not been convicted for an offence against the child, but for some children this will be the case. Where this is the case, then the child needs to know that the person's consequence is to have had choices taken away from them, such as the choice of where they stay and when they leave. They need to know that they will be told when the person is back in the community, and you need to make a safety plan with the child, stressing who will keep them safe and how this will be done. This is because the child may feel very unsafe when they know that the person who hurt them will be back in the community again.

What happens next?

If you are a professional then you will need to think about how to support the family with what happens after prison. It is natural for the family and the prisoner to be focused on the release from custody, with the common perception that everything will be well and good afterwards. We know from experience that this is often not the case. Routines need to be readjusted, boundaries need resetting and families need time to reintegrate. Children are part of this and will have their own perspective and needs. Talking about the issues that are likely to arise with all concerned before the release date, and making a 'coming home' plan, can help a family reintegrate and recognise some of the feelings that arise. The hope is that this empowers them and gives them the opportunity to recognise their needs and access support, if appropriate, in a timely manner.

A 'coming home' plan is really just a simple way to look at the practical things that might cause stress, and try to address these and alleviate them before they happen. With the adults involved it might be about sorting out benefits, or a parent having the opportunity to describe the routine that she has established with the children if it is the other parent in prison. In such a case, both parents will need to think about how the other parent will integrate into this, either in terms of daily routines or perhaps in terms of contact arrangements if the other parent will be living separately. Boundaries should not be forgotten as all children need this, with parents needing to be consistent. There is a tendency for an absent adult to want to spoil a child on return, whether the absence has been through imprisonment, work or a hospital stay. Whilst this is natural and can be a nice experience, it shouldn't last too long or undermine the parent who has been the main carer. The adults should also plan for time alone, as they want and need this. If this is not planned, the children are likely to feel that they are not wanted or are in the way. Where children know in advance that the adults need some time on their own and that they are to stay with another relative perhaps, they will usually accept this.

As a way of getting ready for the family member's return, it can be very useful to involve the children in the 'coming home' plan. They can help decide what should be made for tea the first night, or they might make a banner for the family member. You might want to think about what everyone could do as a family on the first weekend, and plan one-to-one time for each child with the returning adult. This may just be a short time and could be a task such as taking the dog for a walk. However, it is worth planning as this should reduce stress for the child. During this planning phase, adults can prepare the children for the fact that the returning relative might be a bit grumpier than normal. This is usually down to issues around adjustment, but children will tend to assume it is their fault. Warning in advance can help this, but reassurance at the time will still be needed.

Why

It is wise when thinking about what we are going to tell children, to question 'why' at each stage. Why are we telling the child that piece of information? As we spoke about earlier, this work is best done in partnership with a main carer. It is common for the worker to need to gently guide a carer around issues of what to say and how to talk about this sensitive subject. A lot of the people that I work with have faced trauma, poverty and generally harsh circumstances in their lives. Sometimes this means that the way they want to give information to a child, or the content, can feel too harsh or adult. It is relatively rare to find a caregiver whose true intention is to upset or hurt a child, and I have found that the best way to explore this sensitively is to remain curious. So, I commonly say something like, 'That's an interesting point. Can you tell me about why you think it is important that Amy has that piece of information?' Or 'I am wondering why you would say it that way?' It is empowering to encourage the caregiver to ask you 'why' questions as you consider how you will speak to the child. These questions generally lead to a more in-depth discussion and usually result in consensus on what is best for the child.

When

Having a difficult conversation is difficult! Who wouldn't be tempted to put it off? However, it is not a wise move, particularly if children are at an age when they have a sense of time and fairness. With older children, if custody is a possibility, then you may wish to talk to them about all the possible consequences that the sheriff (or judge or jury) could give the adult prior to the court case. The general rule (there will always be exceptions) would be that you should tell the child as soon as you are aware that a custodial sentence has been given. If it is agreed that the child can, and they wish do this, it is helpful to have a date for the first visit or phone call as soon as possible after the child is told of the custodial sentence.

To think in more depth about when, you need to know the child in question. What are their coping mechanisms? What do they find helps when they are upset? It is fair to assume that this news is going to bring about some level of distress, especially if you are informing a child of a parent's imprisonment. Even when a child or young person does not live with the parent, the news that a parent is in prison is very likely going to shake their world. Parents, in children's eyes, are all powerful and invincible and usually have a superhero status. Thus, the realisation that an outside force, that is, the law, can overpower or dominate a parent can be disconcerting and shocking. Even older children will probably struggle with this.

A child who, when given difficult news, likes to almost ignore it for a short while and then come back to talk about it, may be best told just before an activity that will initially distract them. Individual time, set aside with a safe adult with whom they have a good relationship, should be set up for afterwards. A child who needs to go away and play, or be on their own and then come back to ask questions, might be best told on the weekend when they can have space to do this, but can also have access to their main carer. A child who uses peers for support and likes routine might be best told on a school day.

Once you decide on the best timing for the child, consider the support that the caregiver will need. Where there is a competing need (e.g. the weekend would be best for the child but the caregiver then won't have the support of workers who are unavailable), then a compromise will be needed. The child might need to have a day off school to be told, or the caregiver might be supported by telephone through an out-of-hours service.

The following are activities to support discussion around prison:

Activity: Small World Play
Purpose

- To create an opportunity to talk about what will happen/has happened.

- To create an opportunity for a child, through free play, to reflect on and process their experience.

What you will need

- small world toys, for example, Playmobil® or Lego® (Playmobil® and Lego® both do sets based on the police and prison. I recommend these with the proviso that you remove the rather stereotypical prison characters and replace them with ordinary Playmobil®/Lego® characters.)

- some additional arts and crafts material to customise toys if required

- a quiet and comfortable play space where you won't be interrupted.

What to do

1. Before a prison visit you should already have familiarised yourself with the routine of the prison with respect to visitors, which can allow you to play this out with the child. If the sets don't have all that you need, then improvise and make things; for example, the car park or the bus stop where you will get off. Equally, on return, you can play out what happened, choosing a character to be one of the people who the child encountered on their visit. The real value in the introduction of these toys is allowing free play. This provides the child with space to use the toys in the way they wish, and thus an opportunity to explore their feelings.

2. As the adult, your role is to be present with the child and let them know that you are attentive and interested by giving occasional reflections on what they are doing. An example would be, 'I can see you making the policeman drive the big van away' and by helping with any practical problems such as finding what the child needs or separating bricks! However, you should not interfere or lead the play. Sometimes children will invite the adult to play with them; if this happens then go with it but ensure that the child still directs and leads.

3. At times, through this play or afterwards, children will sometimes choose to talk about their feelings and experiences. This will then give the supporting adult the opportunity to actively help. Usually the help will consist of supporting the child emotionally, at times providing information and at times offering the child something practical to do to help them cope with a worry.

Activity: Make Your Own True Story
Purpose

- To allow reflection on the child's life circumstances.

- To check that the child has understood all the facts of their situation.

What you will need

- scrapbook

- good-quality felt tip pens

- glue

- stickers

- access to a computer to type and print words (optional).

What to do

1. Children usually love to make their own story into a book. For younger children, the main carer and you should work out the words for this story. For young children, three lines per page is best. You can invite the child to draw their own picture to illustrate the words, or perhaps cut out pictures. There are various websites for downloading and printing off realistic images. Older children can be encouraged to help the supporting adult in writing the words.

2. Children often want to share these books with teachers or other important people in their life. I would suggest that you warn the adult in question that it is on the way. These little books can be very emotive and so it is helpful if the adult can be prepared and therefore not overwhelmed by the emotion of the moment.

3. Younger children are more likely to also want to share their book with classmates. Children can be understandably proud of their hard work, and can benefit from using it as a voice in talking about something that is emotive and current. Adults, however, can see such matters as private and are likely to want to share such information with as few people as possible. I would suggest that you work with the parent(s)/main carer(s) and school staff to handle this sensitively. It is often helpful to remind people why a child would want to share this information. Adults may project their own values onto

the child, and reservations are sometimes based in shame, or they may wish to protect the child from potentially difficult and hurtful responses from peers. So often children will say to their peers that they are 'not allowed to play' with someone because a parent is in prison/lives in a certain place/uses drugs, etc. Whilst we want to protect children from these difficulties, it is also important that we don't give the child the message that there is shame to their story. I tend to talk about this kind of thing being 'best friend stuff'. This allows the child to tell peers and not to be ashamed of their circumstances, but also to try to teach children to filter how they might give information to the wider group. I do this by getting the child to think about how much they know about someone they are friends with and play with, in comparison to someone they don't play with. From there it is possible to think about the concept of friendship and that stories about family are really for the special people to see. Some children may not have a friendship group and, in this case, I would talk to them about choosing a friend who seems kind. If children's motivation to share a book is about seeking positive attention you may also offer an alternative activity that might achieve the same result. An example might be to bake biscuits for a class, and then invite the child to think about whether they still wish to share the book after this. It won't always work, but may satisfy the need for a child to obtain some positive attention and enable them to think differently about sharing their personal information. Ultimately, however, this is the child's book and therefore the child's choice. Adults need to respect this and support the child no matter what happens. At a later date this book may also be helpful in wider work helping to reflect on the impact this experience had.

Activity: Calendar
Purpose

- To develop a personalised calendar to help the child to track of when the family member is going to be back home. In doing this, the child will gain a sense of control.

What you will need

- string
- pegs
- card
- pens.

Alternatively

- pebbles
- box
- jar.

What to do

1. How this works will depend on the length of the sentence. If, for example, the person was in prison for 6 months, you could mark this by months. Put a string up as you would a washing line, with six pegs on it.

2. In each box, place six pictures with defining things that would happen in the next 6 months. So, if the person was given custody in December, the first picture might be a Christmas tree, you could mark a family birthday month with a cake, another month by a trip you make somewhere such as to the museum or a favourite park.

3. As each activity takes place, the child hangs up that picture on the peg. You should explain to the child that, once all the pegs are full, the family member will be coming home.

4. A bonus of this is that it gives the child a concrete thing to show the family member once home, and to show them what they have doing whilst that person has been in prison. It also promotes the message that it is okay to do pleasant and normal activities whilst the person is in prison, and therefore without them.

There are lots of variations for this activity – for older children they may choose to count out pebbles into a box, one for each week of custody. At the end of each week the box of pebbles can get emptied into a jar, and, once the jar is full, the family member will be home. In this case, you will need to choose a jar that is about the right size to hold however many weeks of pebbles will be accumulated over the custodial time.

PRACTICE EXAMPLE

Whilst as adults we sometimes cross days off on a calendar, in my experience most children find it very daunting to look at, for example, 6 months' worth of calendar. It is more comforting to use objects that can be held and counted at less frequent intervals than daily. For one child I worked with who loved colouring in, I got one of the big tablecloth colouring-in sheets. Her dad was in prison for 6 weeks so I divided the picture into six parts. The idea was that each week she would colour in one part and that, once the picture was fully coloured, her dad would be home. She was 7 years old, and one night she crept downstairs and sat and coloured in the whole sheet, so that her dad would be home sooner.

Whether it was a misunderstanding or wishful thinking, this at least allowed her to express and show how much she missed her dad, and later gave her an opportunity to cry. She herself requested that we wipe clean the 'weeks' that hadn't yet gone by so that she could carry on colouring in for her dad. I also told her dad about this. It was a very real way to demonstrate to him the impact that his offending was having on his child. His usual presentation of cocky confidence changed to quiet contemplation as he stated to me, 'I am not ever coming back here.'

What the family member in prison might do to support the child at home

To a degree this does depend on the particular prison but, in my experience, there is a recognition of the importance of supporting relatives to remain in contact with their children (there are obviously some situations where you would not promote this, but these tend to be the exception). Here are a few ideas of things that you can do.

Record a story

Getting a family member, particularly a parent, to record a story that the child can then listen to is a lovely way for them to stay connected to the child. The barrier to this can be where you have a parent who does not read or perhaps does not feel confident in their reading. The focus is to create a connection between the adult and the child, so looking through a picture book and describing the story that way also works. For the child it is about hearing the family member's voice and being entertained. Children are very forgiving and will love almost any story told to them. The other option is for the family member to tell a story that they can remember from their childhood or perhaps make up a story. Children also enjoy hearing about things that went wrong or a time when the parent was naughty. This could also be done by writing it down. I am a great fan of handwriting as it feels more personal, but a typed letter is also fine, with a hand-written signature and perhaps a little doodle at the end.

Send a collection of pictures

The family member can just cut out pictures from a magazine or use images from a website. They can perhaps choose a theme, such as their favourite animals or cars, or places they grew up, and then write on the back why they have chosen these pictures. Children can then send a collection of pictures back. This activity has the advantage of generating conversation and creating a shared experience, with minimal writing required.

Draw a picture/make a model

This is self-explanatory, but it is a powerful way to stay connected to a child. You don't need to be an artist – a stick person picture will be fine and most prisons will have a craft/art area, often with the chance to access an art teacher.

Photos/hand prints

It may be tricky for the person in prison to provide a photo but I would hope that the child can be provided or have access to photos of the absent family member. They might enjoy it being in a frame in their room but others will prefer to have it in an album that they can keep with them. Ask the child what they would prefer.

A hand print is a lovely thing for the family member in prison to do for the child. My favoured way of doing this is to provide a piece of air drying clay. You roll this out until it is about 2 cm thick. The person presses their hand into it leaving an imprint (you need to press down quite hard so a steady table is a must). The person can then write messages around the hand print using a blunt pencil to write into the clay. Leave the clay to dry out slowly and then wrap it in special paper and place it in a box, with a message such as, 'When you want to hold my hand, you can place your hand in mine. Love and hugs from…' or, for a younger child, you could write, 'My hand print. You can touch it when you miss me. Love and hugs from…' I did have a situation where I was not allowed to bring clay into the prison. In that case, a hand print using paint onto paper and then placing that in an envelope can work as well.

TV/shared activity

For slightly older children, the family member and child could agree to watch a particular TV programme at the same time or possibly another shared activity such as reading the same book (Harry Potter springs to mind! Loved by all ages!). The aim of this is to give the feeling of being connected, with a special time when both are doing the same thing and thinking of each other. It also means that during visits or phone calls there is a shared experience to talk about. Children can often become quite fixed on this, which is a reflection of how it is important to them and is having the desired effect. However, this being the case, you need to ensure that the child's main carer is supportive of this activity, as there will be tantrums and tears if the child is for, whatever reason, prevented from watching that programme. This can be quite a commitment to take on, to ensure that the child can see it each day/week it is on.

A little box of words

Parents in particular often have affectionate things that they say to their children, whether a nickname or a phrase that they regularly repeat to their children. Write these down and put them in a small decorated box. You could use a matchbox that has been wrapped and coloured in (by the parent perhaps) or a small tin. This can then be placed under the child's pillow or in another safe but accessible place chosen by the child. The child can then look at this whenever they wish. Younger children may need support to read this, and may need prompting at particular moments to look at this. For example, 'I wonder what do you think [name of person] would say? Why don't you go and bring your word box?'

Prison visits

The key to planning for these is to know your prison! As mentioned above, using small world toys in preparation can be helpful, particularly for children under 10 years old. Asking the prison for printed information is worthwhile. Edinburgh Prison, for example, has a really well-illustrated leaflet for children about visiting. The way to reduce stress for children is to make sure that they know what to expect. Detail is important, including things like the fact that all the prisoners will wear the same clothes, that the individual won't be able to just get up and walk about, explaining the level of physical contact that is allowed and warning them about the length of the visit. During the visit, expect the child to be shy or wary at first and warn the person in custody that this likely to happen. It is not a reflection of them or their relationship with the child but rather a normal response to a different environment. The best plan is to just reassure the child and then ignore this presentation, with adults leading the conversation for a few minutes. Don't be surprised if this happens on every visit, though I would suggest that it should lessen as time goes on. Encourage the child to ask questions. Also, give them a countdown to the ending, for example, we have 10 minutes, 5 minutes, and take the time to talk about it afterwards. The person in custody may well feel overwhelmed during the child's visit. Most people will try to contain this so as not to upset the child. However, inevitably there will be times when people are overwhelmed. It is important not to shy away from talking about these very real emotions with children. You perhaps would start by acknowledging what is happening, for example, 'Mummy is sad because she is missing you' or 'Daddy was upset because he wanted to leave with us but he is not allowed to.' Doing this helps the child to put into words what they have witnessed and gives them permission to talk about it. Be prepared to stay with the child in their emotion, whatever this is. This isn't always an easy place to stay in so remember to access support for yourself afterwards.

It is important that children know when the next contact will be, whether by phone or by a visit, or both. If when they leave, the person appears upset, both reassure that the prison officer will care for the person/the person will be okay, and give the child a practical thing to do. You might, for example, suggest that the child draws the person a picture when they get home, so that you can post it and cheer that person up.

Children should never be forced to visit someone in prison and, even if they are willing to visit and appear happy during the visit, adults must observe the impact of the contact before, during and after. If there is an indication that this is causing the child significant distress, a decision to stop taking the child on prison visits might need to be made. At all times, the child's welfare must be given priority.

Chapter 18

Looking After Yourself

It is always important to recognise the impact this type of work has on the helping/supporting adults. In order to maintain your own emotional health – and thus allow you to continue to offer others care – you must attend to it.

Give yourself time to reflect, process the emotions raised and understand your own responses. Social workers are offered regular supervision to do this, but if you don't have a system in place such as supervision then consider who the appropriate person would be in your workplace to seek support from. If you are a family member it is important to seek support from either informal or formal channels, particularly if you are processing a difficult situation for yourself, alongside supporting the child.

As a supervisee, you have the responsibility to bring such issues to supervision. Informally there will ideally be support from colleagues but this does not replace supervision, though it can complement it. It also can provide an immediate opportunity to share some of the emotion or stress. This can be a real advantage to everyone working well together in a child care team.

Also be aware that our own personal lives can be such that situations at work may trigger difficult things for ourselves. Many of the issues discussed in this book are relatively uncommon and it may be that we have had, or are still facing, similar issues in our personal life. Where possible, it can be helpful for a supervisor to be aware that this is an issue, in order for you to be supported more effectively.

We asked some of our colleagues to give us examples of what helps them to manage their stress when working with families experiencing difficulties.

How do you deal with the emotions that your job brings?

I always make sure I have a good book on the go! Even reading it for 5 minutes in the car at lunchtime can reduce my stress levels enormously.

I have a plan for Friday nights – eat a takeaway and do nothing.

My husband is a police officer and I am a social worker mostly doing child protection work. When we get home, we have an hour's work talk and then we stop. It is a firm rule in our house.

I like to work a little bit away from home – there is a reason for that. My car time is my wind down time from work. When I go in, I go straight for a shower and change out of my work clothes – once I am in home clothes, I switch off.

If it's all getting too much I find a colleague and talk about it – works for me every time.

Sometimes it is hard to remember some children have happy lives. If I am struggling to remember that I go and see my nephew.

I do a sporting activity that requires a lot of concentration. When I am there, I therefore can't think of anything else except what I am doing. It's an amazing escape for my mind and my body is busy releasing hormones that are associated with feeling positive.

Appendix

Worry Characters

References

Department of Justice (2017) *Experience of Domestic Violence: Findings from the 2011/12 to 2015/16 Northern Ireland Crime Surveys.* Accessed on 19/08/2017 at: www.justice-ni.gov.uk/sites/default/files/publications/justice/experience-of-domestic-violence-findings-201112-201516-northern-rreland-crime-surveys.pdf.

Ironside, V. (2011) *The Huge Bag of Worries.* Sydney: Hodder Children's Books.

Kerr, J. (2004) *Mog on Fox Night.* London: Harper Collins.

Office for National Statistics (2016) *Intimate Personal Violence and Partner Abuse.* Accessed on 19/08/2017 at: www.ons.gov.uk/peoplepopulationandcommunity/crimeandjustice/compendium/focusonviolentcrimeandsexualoffences/yearendingmarch2015/chapter4intimatepersonalviolenceandpartnerabuse#prevalence-of-intimate-violence-extent.

Prince, M., Wimo, A., Guerchet, M., Ali, G., Wu, Y. and Prina, M. (2015) *World Alzheimer Report 2015: The Global Impact of Dementia.* London: Alzheimer's Disease International.

Royal College of Psychiatrists (2017) *Problems and Disorders Index.* Accessed on 18/09/2017 at: http://rcpsych.ac.uk/healthadvice/problemsdisorders.aspx.

Ross, D. (2001) *I Fought at Bannockburn.* Glasgow: Waverly Books Ltd.

Scottish Government (2016) *Scottish Crime and Justice Survey 2014/5: Partner Abuse* [online]. Accessed on 19/08/2017 at: www.gov.scot/Publications/2016/05/2505.

Tait, A. and Wosu, H. (2012) *Direct Work with Vulnerable Children.* London: Jessica Kingsley Publishers.

Tait, A. and Wosu, H. (2015) *Direct Work with Family Groups.* London: Jessica Kingsley Publishers.

Turnell, A. and Essex, S. (2006) *Working with Situations of 'Denied' Child Abuse: The Resolutions Approach.* Buckingham: Open University Press.

Van Gulden, H. and Vick, C. (2005) *Learning the Dance of Attachment.* Minneapolis, MN: Adoptive Family Counseling Center.

Direct Work with Family Groups Simple, Fun Ideas to Aid Engagement and Assessment and Enable Positive Change
Audrey Tait and Helen Wosu

Paperback: £16.99/$29.95
ISBN: 978 1 84905 554 3
eISBN: 978 0 85700 986 9
216 pages

Direct Work with Family Groups is full of great ideas to aid engagement, assessment and enable positive change.

Working with families can be a challenging experience. This book looks at the personal skills needed to engage families, both at home and in the community. It provides guidance on how to assess and manage the needs of individual family members, whilst also being mindful of potential risk factors. With easy-to-use activities and resources, this book will inspire you to think about creative new ways to plan and carry out your work.

Based on tried and tested techniques, this is a must-have for social workers and social work students, as well as child protection workers, therapists, counsellors and child and family centre workers. It is the perfect complement to Direct Work with Vulnerable Children, also by the same authors.

Helen Wosu is an independent Social Worker and holds an MSc in Advanced Social Work Practice from the University of Edinburgh. She currently undertakes kinship care assessments as well as child development and child protection training.

Direct Work with Vulnerable Children
Playful Activities and Strategies for Communication
Audrey Tait and Helen Wosu

Paperback: £16.99/$29.95
ISBN: 978 1 84905 319 8
224 pages

For many vulnerable children, the idea of talking to an adult about their experiences and feelings can be a daunting prospect. This book demonstrates how the introduction of playfulness when working with neglected or abused children helps to build a trusting relationship by openly engaging with the child's world.

The practical activities and resources provided have been developed over 20 years of working with vulnerable children and are proven to help reduce feelings of stress and open up the lines of communication between adult and child. The straightforward, accessible style makes them easy to follow and ideal for reference in everyday practice.

With plenty of tried and tested advice, this book is essential reading for all those working with vulnerable children, including social workers, child protection workers, therapists, teachers and police interviewers, who are looking for effective ways to engage with them.

A Therapeutic Treasure Deck of Feelings and Sentence Completion Cards
Dr. Karen Treisman

Cards: £22.99/$29.95
ISBN: 978 1 78592 398 2
68 cards and booklet

The perfect tool to add to any 'therapeutic treasure box', this set of 68 cards provide a way to help open conversations and structure discussions with children and adolescents aged 6+.

The treasure deck offers a fun, non-threatening way to help to build understanding and forge relationships. It also provides a safe, playful way for children to articulate and make sense of their feelings, thoughts, experiences and beliefs. The deck comes with two different types of card - the 'feelings cards' and the 'sentence-completion cards' - which can be used separately or together, and the cards are accompanied by a booklet which explains some of the different ways in which they can be therapeutically used.

Designed and tested by specialist clinical psychologist, trainer and author Dr Karen Treisman, this deck is a little treasure that will have great value for anyone working with children and adolescents aged 6+.

Dr. Karen Treisman is a specialist clinical psychologist, trainer, and author, working in London, UK. Karen is also the Director of Safe Hands and Thinking Minds Training and Consultancy services.